This is a continuation in the series of publications produced by the Center for Advanced Concepts and Technology (ACT), which was created as a "skunk works" with funding provided by the CCRP under the auspices of the Assistant Secretary of Defense (C3I). This program has demonstrated the importance of having a research program focused on the national security implications of the Information Age. It develops the theoretical foundations to provide DoD with information superiority and highlights the importance of active outreach and dissemination initiatives designed to acquaint senior military personnel and civilians with these emerging issues. The CCRP Publication Series is a key element of this effort.

Check our website for the latest CCRP activities and publications.

www.dodccrp.org

DoD C4ISR Cooperative Research Program

ASSISTANT SECRETARY OF DEFENSE (C3I)

Mr. Arthur L. Money

SPECIAL ASSISTANT TO THE ASD(C3I)
&
DIRECTOR, RESEARCH AND STRATEGIC PLANNING

Dr. David S. Alberts

Library of Congress Cataloging-in-Publication Data

Alberts, David S. (David Stephen), 1942-
    Network centric warfare : developing and leveraging information superiority /
  David S. Alberts, John J. Garstka, Frederick P. Stein.
       p.   cm. -- (CCRP publication series)
    Includes bibliographical references.
    ISBN 1-57906-019-6
    1. Military art and science--Forecasting. 2. War--Forecasting.
  3. Information technology. 4. Command and control systems.
  5. Twenty-first century--Forecasts. I. Garstka, John. II. Stein,
  Frederick P. III. Title. IV. Series.
  U21.2.A413 1999
  355.02'09'05--dc21   98-53271
  2nd Edition (Revised)   CIP
  August 1999
  Special reprint by Sun Microsystems Federal, Inc.
  February 2000

We're the dot in .com™

NETWORK CENTRIC WARFARE:

Developing and Leveraging Information Superiority

2nd Edition (Revised)

David S. Alberts
John J. Garstka
Frederick P. Stein

Table of Contents

List of Figures

Acknowledgments

This book is the product of an ongoing effort to understand and articulate the power of information superiority in warfare from a Joint perspective. This work would not have been possible without the support, encouragement, and cooperation of ASD(C3I) and the J6. We would like to acknowledge the direct and substantive contributions by: Vice Admiral Arthur K. Cebrowski, USN; LTG Douglas D. Buchholz, USA (Retired); and Lt Gen John L. Woodward, USAF. Many individuals have worked with us on numerous drafts. Included among those who have contributed comments and suggestions that have greatly enhanced this book are (in alphabetical order): Chuck Bartlett, John Dickmann, Roy Evans, James FitzSimonds, Dean Free, Dick Hayes, John Hodell, Leland Joe, Kevin Kirsch, Margaret Myers, Nick Petronzio, Paul Romanski, Dan Ryan, Stu Starr, Mark Tempestilli, and Gary Wheatley.

We owe a huge debt of thanks to Margita Rushing for her work on draft after draft and to Meg Rittler for her artistic treatment on most of the figures and the cover design.

Finally, the authors deeply appreciate the opportunity to write this book and the forbearance of our families who saw less of us as a result.

Preface

It will be decades before the real book on Network Centric Warfare will be written. This effort is designed to help prepare for the journey that will take us from an emerging concept to the fielding of real operational capability. The success of any journey depends in great measure upon the preparations made. These preparations include a shared sense of purpose, a destination, education and training, and provisions. Many challenges remain. One that is already causing problems is not having a concrete destination, but rather a broad vision of the characteristics of the destination. In a journey such as this, the process becomes the concrete objective for those who are guided by a vision. It is hoped that this book will contribute to the preparations for this journey in two ways. First, by articulating the nature of the characteristics of Network Centric Warfare (NCW). Second, by suggesting a process for developing mission capability packages designed to transform NCW concepts into operational capabilities. The CCRP is continuing to work with others to undertake research and outreach initiatives aimed at developing a better understanding of network-centric concepts and their application to national security. We are interested in hearing about your efforts and ideas.

Given the velocity of the evolution of ideas and experiences about NCW, it is impossible for a "print media" to keep up. Consequently, we find ourselves literally updating and expanding the material in this manuscript from the moment it left on its journey to the "presses." While we may in the future publish an updated edition, readers should visit the CCRP website at www.dodccrp.org for updated versions and additional material on the subject.

David S. Alberts
Director, Research OASD(C3I)

Introduction

War is a product of its age. The tools and tactics of how we fight have always evolved along with technology. We are poised to continue this trend.[1]

Warfare in the Information Age will inevitably embody the characteristics that distinguish this age from previous ones. These characteristics affect the capabilities that are brought to battle as well as the nature of the environment in which conflicts occur.

Often in the past, military organizations pioneered both the development of technology and its application. Such is not the case today. Major advances in Information Technology are being driven primarily by the demands of the commercial sector. Furthermore, Information Technology is being applied commercially in ways that are transforming business around the globe.

The purposes of this book are to describe the Network Centric Warfare concept; to explain how it embodies the characteristics of the Information Age; to identify the challenges in transforming this concept into a real operational capability; and to suggest a prudent approach to meeting these challenges.

In the commercial sector, dominant competitors have developed information superiority and translated it into a competitive advantage by making the shift to network-centric operations. They have accomplished this by exploiting information technology and coevolving their organizations and processes to provide their customers with more value. The coevolution of organization and process is being powered by a number of mutually reinforcing, rapidly emerging trends that link information technology and increased competitiveness.

Similar concepts are beginning to take root in military thinking, new concepts, plans, and experiments. It is for this reason that developments in the commercial sector are significant and worthy of note, for they provide insights into the potential power of information superiority in the conduct of military operations.

Network Centric Warfare is the best term developed to date to describe the way we will organize and fight in the Information Age. The Chief of Naval Operations, Admiral Jay Johnson, has called it "a fundamental shift from platform-centric warfare."[2] We define NCW as an information superiority-enabled concept of operations that generates increased combat power by networking sensors, decision makers, and shooters to achieve shared awareness, increased speed of command, higher tempo of operations, greater lethality, increased survivability, and a degree of self-synchronization. In essence, NCW translates information superiority into combat power by effectively linking knowledgeable entities in the battlespace.

Joint Vision 2010's (JV2010) parallels to the revolution in the commercial sector are striking, with JV2010's stated emphasis on developing information superiority and translating it to increased combat power across the spectrum of operations, as well as the key role of experimentation in enabling coevolution of organization and doctrine.

To reach its full potential, Network Centric Warfare must be deeply rooted in operational art. As such, we cannot simply apply new technologies to the current platforms, organizations, and doctrine of warfare. There is ample historical precedence for the coevolution of organization, doctrine, and technology in the warfighting ecosystem. For example, performance advantages at the platform level have often led to the emergence of new doctrine, tactics, techniques, or procedures. During World War II, Army Air Corps commanders increased the survivability and lethality of daylight bombing operations by coevolving tactics to exploit the improved range and endurance capabilities of the P-51 and the improved capabilities of the Norden Bombsight to conduct daylight precision bombing with fighter protection for the otherwise more vulnerable bombers.[34] Similarly, coevolution played a key role in the eventual Allied victory in the Battle of Britain. In this decisive air campaign, the introduction of radar coupled with the change it enabled in the command and control structure and system provided Allies with a critical competitive advantage.[5] Consequently, as we continue to apply emerging information technologies, we should not be surprised by the need to explore new warfighting concepts that employ new organizations or new processes.

Different organizations have different time constraints with respect to change. Within the private sector there are many organizations in the vanguard of a shift to network-centric operations. These organizations provide us with a look into a possible future. We need to closely examine the experiences of these organizations and if they are applicable, apply the lessons learned.

We set the stage with a discussion of the myths currently circulating about NCW; a description of the nature of the changes taking place in the commercial sector, and a discussion of their implications for military organizations and operations. The concept of NCW is then introduced and reviewed in detail. Given the profound implications for how the military organizes, equips, trains, and fights, we then address the process by which technology is introduced into organizations. The book concludes with a discussion of the road ahead and a strategy for moving from NCW-based concepts to NCW-based operations.

Since successful adoption of NCW requires a cultural change, it cannot be achieved without widespread discussion, debate, experimentation, and ultimately, broad acceptance. If this book stimulates and contributes to this process, it will have achieved its intended effect.

NCW Myths

We are sure that many readers have already read a lot and heard a lot about Network Centric Warfare (NCW). Certainly there is no shortage of exaggerated claims, unfounded criticisms, and just plain misinformation about this subject. Sorting out fact from fancy will be among the community's principal tasks as we grapple with how to apply network-centric concepts to military operations. The following discussion of a number of myths currently circulating about the nature, limitations, and dangers of Network Centric Warfare will set the stage for the detailed exploration of Network Centric Warfare concepts offered here. It will do so by alerting the reader to a number of important issues that must be addressed and widely understood if we are to achieve the critical mass of consensus needed to rapidly move ahead.

The Myths

Myth 1: We are experts on NCW and this book has all of the answers.

The truth is that we are not experts on NCW and far more importantly, in our opinion, no one is. In fact at the current time, NCW is far more a state of mind than a concrete reality. Despite this, scattered evidence is now beginning to emerge in the form of "existence proofs" that document the value-added provided by NCW capabilities. These are referenced in later sections. This book will be only one of many attempts to understand and explain the concepts of NCW and their application to specific military organizations and operations. It will be some time before the full potential of NCW concepts will be understood and even more time before we begin to realize their potential. We need to move beyond bumper stickers to fully explore and debate this important subject. It is our hope that this book will stimulate and contribute to such a discourse, helping to make all of us more aware of the potentials and pitfalls of NCW.

Translating this concept into a real operational capability requires far more than just injecting information technology in the form of an information infrastructure or *infostructure*. It requires concepts of operation, C2 approaches, organizational forms, doctrine, force structure, support services and the like—all working together to leverage the available information. We call this a Mission Capability Package (MCP). How NCW concepts will ultimately be manifested in Mission Capability Packages designed to leverage Information Superiority is the central question we all face. The answer, despite premature predictions to the contrary, will unfold only after much hard work.

Myth 2: NCW is all about the network.

Actually, NCW is more about networking than networks. It is about the increased combat power that can be generated by a network-centric force. As we will show, the power of NCW is derived from the effective linking or networking of knowledgeable entities that are geographically or hierarchically dispersed. The networking of knowledgeable entities enables them to share information and collaborate to develop shared awareness, and also to collaborate with one another to achieve a degree of self-synchronization. The net result is increased combat power.

Myth 3: NCW will change the nature of warfare.

Obviously, the word nature means different things to different people, but if you take a look at the principles of war, only the principles of mass and maneuver need to be somewhat reinterpreted to reflect the massing of effects, not forces. The other principles remain as meaningful as ever.

NCW does however offer us an opportunity to improve our ability to achieve these principles by reducing the tensions among them. We will show that the principles related to the offense, economy of force, surprise, and unity of command can clearly be helped by the application of NCW concepts. And despite some well-founded concern, we believe NCW can also contribute to achieving the principle of simplicity.

Myth 4: NCW applies only to large-scale conflict with a peer competitor.

If one associates NCW with the kind of tactical sensor-to-shooter low hanging fruit that early experiments are focusing on, then one might be tempted to reach this conclusion. However, if one takes a look at the principles of war, which apply pretty broadly across the mission spectrum, then one is forced to conclude otherwise.

For example, the principle of offensive is to act rather than react and to dictate the time, place, purpose, scope, intensity, and pace of operations. This is all about battlespace awareness, speed of command, and responsiveness. As will be demonstrated later in this book, the application of NCW concepts has enormous potential for improving our ability to achieve battlespace awareness, speed of command, and force responsiveness. We will also show that the application of NCW concepts have proven useful in Operations Other Than War (OOTW) including *Desert Fox*, *Deliberate Force*, and in Bosnia.

While it is true that our collection systems are not currently designed for OOTW, this does not negate the promise that NCW has for improving upon our current approaches to these kinds of operations. Thus, rather than saying that NCW is not applicable to OOTW, it would be more accurate to say that we could not hope to fully realize the promise of NCW without proper attention to the collection and analysis of appropriate information. But even in the case where information is far less than perfect, it could reasonably be argued that being able to have a shared understanding of what is known and what is not known would be preferable to a situation in which units operated in isolated ignorance.

Myth 5: NCW makes us more vulnerable to asymmetric attacks.

We are, of course, far too vulnerable for comfort. We cannot tell you NCW will make us less vulnerable. The truth is that nobody knows. This is because it depends on how the concepts of NCW are translated into concepts of operation, doctrine, force structure, and each of the other elements that comprise a mission capability package. Our increasing dependence on our "system of systems" and our potential vulnerabilities to problems like Y2K, information warfare, or simply malfunctions due to sheer complexity should give us pause. These vulnerability issues need to be more fully explored as the number of our systems and our dependence upon their proper functioning continues to grow and as they individually and collectively become more complex.

However, it would be foolish to discard the concept of NCW because of these concerns. Rather we need to keep our vulnerabilities in mind as we proceed to define and build our future infostructure and take steps to rigorously test proposed NCW solutions, subjecting them to information attacks.

Myth 6: We are already well on the road to NCW.

To fully leverage Information Superiority and apply the concepts of NCW to the full range of tasks we in DoD undertake in support of our many mission challenges, two things are required—first, a suitable infostructure and second, coevolved mission capability packages.

While we are taking steps in the right direction, and indeed are making useful progress, unless we take appropriate action now, we will fall short in both areas, hampering our ability to make further progress. First, the infostructure we can reasonably expect, given current plans, investments, and acquisition processes will have shortfalls in several significant dimensions. We can expect continued vulnerabilities, a lack of connectivity and bandwidth, particularly for that stubborn last mile, and problems with mobility and survivability. One problem we grapple with is the program-centric way we acquire capabilities. Another is the need for improved approaches to the challenges associated with integrating a federation of systems.

Second, unless we do a better job of nurturing and rewarding innovation, our applications of NCW concepts are more likely to be linear extensions of current concepts and practices rather than being truly innovative. We may be thus trapped in a vicious cycle, where a lack of infostructure will hamper the ability of innovators by making it difficult to imagine what is possible and to test out new ideas, and by making the concepts that are developed seem beyond reach.

Myth 7: The commercial world has shown us the way, all we need to do is follow.

In fact, network-centric concepts do not automatically translate into effective organizations. This is true whether or not one is trying to apply this concept in the commercial sector or to DoD. This assertion that "what is good for business is good for DoD" is a dangerous oversimplification. However, the converse assertion that "lessons learned in the commercial sector have no application to the domain of warfare" is equally untrue and if believed, would deny us an opportunity to learn from the experiences of others when they are applicable.

Myth 8: NCW will give us the power to dominate our adversaries.

Obviously, anyone that claims that NCW concepts are "the answer" clearly misunderstands what NCW is all about. As we will show, NCW allows us to get the most out of our people and our assets. However, better awareness depends upon not only sharing what we know but also upon our ability to collect and analyze needed information. Improved collaboration, speed of command, and other attributes of command and control will not make up for weapons that are insufficient or inappropriate for the task at hand. Thus, it is important to remember that we need balanced mission capability packages to satisfy our operational warfighting requirements.

There are some types of operations that we are not as well equipped to do as others. Clearly, in some of these cases we need to invest in other capabilities in order to make significant gains. Thus, while NCW has the potential to improve upon current performance, it is clearly not a panacea.

Myth 9: NCW will not survive first contact with the real fog, friction, and complexity of war.

The fact that warfare will always be characterized by fog, friction, complexity, and irrationality circumscribes but does not negate the benefits that network-centric operations can provide to the forces in terms of improved battlespace awareness and access to distributed assets. While predicting human and organizational behavior will remain well beyond the state of the art, having a better near real-time picture of what is happening (in situations where this is possible from observing things that move, emit, etc.) certainly reduces uncertainty in a meaningful way. We would argue that better battlespace awareness and increased responsiveness could help us shape the battle to our advantage. This notion is not new, but an extension of the classic principal of offensive. NCW concepts hold the promise of giving us more to work with.

Myth 10: NCW is an attempt to automate war that can only fail.

NCW is not about turning the battle over to "the network" or even about relying more on automated tools and decision aids. It is really about exploiting information to maximize combat power by bringing more of our available information and warfighting assets to bear both effectively and efficiently. NCW is about developing collaborative working environments for commanders, and indeed for all our soldiers, sailors, marines, and airmen to make it easier to develop common perceptions of the situation and achieve (self-) coordinated responses to situations. However, there is definitely a place for automated tools and decision aids on the battlespaces of the future. As we will explain, there are different types of decisions to be made and different tools and approaches to these decisions are appropriate. Potentially, a lot could be gained from the prudent application of automated processes—arguments *ad absurdum* not withstanding.

Myth 11: NCW will result in our chasing our tails rather than responding to battlespace events.

There has been some concern voiced about NCW's effect on the speed of command. The worry is that we will develop a pace that is so rapid that we will "get ahead of ourselves" on the battlefield, responding not to an adversary's actions and reactions, but to ourselves (chasing our tails, as it were). Obviously, one can easily construct situations and circumstances where "speed of command" is irrelevant or worse, harmful. But there are many circumstances and missions where, all things being equal, speed of command will be decisive. The point is that NCW gives us an opportunity to increase speed of command when it is appropriate; it does not force us to do so when it is not. Thus, the point we can take away is the need to better understand how we can leverage speed of command in military situations and dispel the myth that speed (or any other single factor) is either a panacea or an unmitigated good.

Summary

It is important to realize that each of these myths contains the germ of a valid concern. It would be unfortunate if, because of the way in which these concerns are expressed, they were not given due attention as we proceed on our journey into the future.

The Information Age

Recent advances in Information Technologies (IT) and the ability of organizations and individuals to take advantage of the opportunities these advances provide are profoundly altering the nature of the world in which we live. The Information Age is:

1) changing how wealth is created;
2) altering the distribution of power;
3) increasing the complexity;
4) shrinking distances around the world; and
5) compressing time, which increases the tempo of our lives.

This chapter examines the nature of those changes.

The Technology

Information Technology is the DNA of the Information Age—the fundamental building block of dominant competitors. The underlying trends in Information Technology (which are discussed in Appendix A) are coalescing to create *orders of magnitude increases* in the ability of human beings to operate in the information domain. At the most basic level, the primary observable of this quantum improvement in the information domain can be observed in the dimensions of speed and access.

Across a broad range of activities and operations, the time required by individuals to access or collect the information relevant to a decision or action has been reduced by orders of magnitude, while the volume of information that can be accessed has increased exponentially. In some competitive domains, the timelines for creating value have been reduced from hours to seconds (e.g., on-line trading). Consequently, across a broad range of value-creating activities, the fundamental limits to the velocity of operations are no longer governed by space or time. Instead, the fundamental limits are governed by the act of deciding, by the firings of neurons, by the speed of thought.

Clearly, these revolutionary changes in the information domain have the potential to have the same level of impact on the fabric of society that previous revolutionary technologies have wrought (e.g., the steam engine, the internal combustion engine, the airplane). These changes created new opportunities for creating and distributing wealth and power. At this phase of the Information Age, it is clear that we are poised to continue compressing time and space beyond the physical limits ofthe Industrial Age.

Wealth and Power

The original recipe for wealth creation featured land, labor, and capital as its key ingredients. In the Industrial Age the relative importance of land diminished as factories required mainly capital and labor. Capital was needed for machinery and raw materials. The demand for labor, still needed for production, abated somewhat as productivity increased.

Creating wealth involves adding value, turning raw ingredients into products. Energy in one form or another is required to accomplish this transformation. Our progression from one age to another has been propelled by a change in the source of energy, freeing us from former constraints and making energy more available and less expensive. In the Age of Agriculture, primarily humans and beasts of burden supplied energy. Steam, the combustion engine, and electricity derived from a variety of fossil fuels fueled the Industrial Age. Later, nuclear energy was added to the mix. In the early stages of the Information Age, we continue to use large quantities of the fuels associated with past ages, but as technology advances, we require less and less power and hence less of the traditional fuels to accomplish a given task.[6]

The explosive growth in wealth and the changes in its distribution we are experiencing in the Information Age are being driven by three factors. All involve information, one as a product, one as a raw material, and the third as a fuel.

The nature of the product mix has changed over time. Products were once exclusively a mix of natural materials with minimal processing (e.g., food, fibers, stone, and wood). This changed to a mix that was dominated by invented and manufactured products. Information and intellectual property are now playing increasingly important roles as their percentage of the mix increases. The importance of information as a raw material will increase with the proliferation of products that are manufactured from information. These information products serve as fuel for other enterprises in the processes that add value to their raw materials. There is hardly an enterprise anywhere that does not increasingly rely on information products to keep abreast of its competition or to make itself more productive. Many organizations now devote significant amounts of resources to collect and mine the information that is integral in their day-to-day operations (e.g., using the information collected by point-of-sale scanners to understand the buying habits of customers). Others subscribe to a variety of information services whose aim is to reduce uncertainty. Information is playing an increasingly important role in the processes that add value to raw materials, whether these raw materials are in the traditional sense animal, mineral, or vegetable or whether the raw material is ideas.

In some enterprises, information is the main raw material, the predominant fuel, and the product (e.g., information services such as Bloomberg and Reuters). In Information Age factories, products such as software, once developed, can be duplicated and distributed at very low marginal costs. Ideas, always important, now for the first time can result in the creation of wealth without a substantial capital investment.

Wealth and power have always been closely interrelated, with significant capital being necessary to obtain the instruments of power (weapons and armies). Today's world is, in some ways, a far more dangerous place because more players can afford the investments needed for weapons of mass destruction (WMD) and terror. The affordability of WMD is reaching a level where they are no longer the exclusive property of nation states. They can now be increasingly found in the arsenals of terrorists, financed by rogue states or even wealthy individuals. The advent of Information Warfare exacerbates the problem. The tools and techniques of information war are even less expensive and more widely available than the traditional WMD. Moreover, the havoc they could wreak is not yet fully understood. Imagine what would have happened if tanks, planes, ships, and munitions could be copied and distributed like software. The platforms and weapons of information warfare can.[7]

But weapons are not the only instruments of power. Information, as it has often been said, is power. But when this expression was coined, information (like WMD) was a relatively rare, expensive, and restricted commodity. This saying is more applicable today than ever, but in a different sense. Information technologies are greatly improving our ability to collect and store data, process and analyze it to create information, and distribute it widely. Information is being transformed from a relatively rare product into a plentiful one; being turned from an expensive commodity into an inexpensive one; and being freed from the control of a few to make it almost universally accessible.

The increasing availability and affordability of information, information technologies, and Information Age weapons increases the potential for creating formidable foes from impotent adversaries.

This explosion of information is affecting the distribution of power among and within societies, both democratic and autocratic alike, by increasing public awareness. Not only are people more aware of what is going on and of views that may not conform to those of their governments, but the governments are more aware of what the people are thinking. All of this is happening in real time. Fewer and fewer governments can risk the loss of public support. Thus, we are seeing a shift of power to the people unequaled in history.[8]

In a parallel movement, more organizations and institutions are becoming international and transnational as the Information Age has reduced the importance of location and contributed to the process of globalization. The interests of these organizations are becoming less aligned with those of particular governments. Taking sides in conflicts between countries is usually not in these organizations' self-interest. This also represents a shift in the distribution of power, creating more players on the world stage.

Complexity, Time, and Space

The proliferation of significant players and the global nature of markets and economies are increasing the complexity of doing business, whether that business is in the public or private sectors. Complexity is increasing in large part due to the impact that the Information Age is having on the dimensions of time and space.

The Information Age is making distance less relevant. Information, and the decisions that result, can travel almost instantaneously to the place(s) where they are needed, making the location of those who gather, analyze, make decisions, and possibly those who act on these decisions, largely irrelevant.

The Information Age is also compressing the time dimension. First, by making location less important, it reduces the need for time-consuming travel, whether local or long distance. Second, to the extent that information gathering, analysis, and decision making are activities on the critical path, advances in Information Age concepts and technologies are compressing process cycle time. The intensity of these effects is more pronounced in the many processes where information is playing an increasingly important role.[9]

These changes in the dimensions of time and space are increasing the pace of events, or operating tempo, in many different environments. This phenomenon is seen in the rapid fluctuations of the stock market around the world, in the shortening half-life of a breaking news story, in the shrinking time it takes for a product to reach the market, and in the waning attention span of the public. Responsiveness and agility are fast becoming the critical attributes for organizations hoping to survive and prosper in the Information Age.

In the Darwinian world of business, those organizations that are emerging as winners are those that can be described as being *information enabled*. These organizations have found ways to leverage the available information and make the right decisions and right products quickly and efficiently.

The emergence and ascendancy of information-enabled organizations is the result of coevolution in the domain of business. Coevolution, in the sense we use it in this book, is derived from the Santa Fe Institute's research into complex adaptive systems. Biologists have observed that over a large number of life times, species coevolve with each other. We apply this logical construct to the domain of warfare where concepts of operation coevolve in response to changes in their ecosystem.[10] These changes can be quite diverse and include changes in the geopolitical landscape, social and economic changes, changes in the nature of the threat, and advances in technology. In the domain of warfare these ecosystem changes serve to stimulate a series of interrelated changes in concepts of operation, doctrine, organization, command and control approaches, systems, education, training, and people. All these elements come together to form mission capability packages designed for specific tasks and missions.

Summary

Even at this early stage of the Information Age, we are experiencing profound changes in the nature of our world. Wealth and power, for so long the providence of the few, are being created with new time constants and distributed far more widely. For example, it is now possible for entrepreneurs behind successful Internet-based companies (e.g., Yahoo, Amazon.com, and eBay) to become billionaires in periods measured in months, and for the public to share in this value-creation process.11 This is creating a plethora of significant new players. Among these are the public who have been empowered by information; transnational organizations that have been created by the phenomenon of globalization; and a host of state and non-state adversaries made more dangerous by the proliferation of the instruments of power, including WMD and Information Warfare. The Information Age has also resulted in greatly increased complexity arising out of a need to deal with more players and at a much faster operating tempo.

Information Age
Organizations

Commercial organizations are leading the way in adopting Information Age concepts and technologies and in adapting to a changing world. These organizations are being driven by a need to keep abreast of invigorated competition, facilitated by the lowering of barriers to entry and by the elimination, or reduction, in the competitive advantage that established organizations have developed and held for some time. These incumbent advantages have been eroded by changes in cost structures, methods of production and distribution, and characteristics of the marketplace resulting from the introduction of Information Age concepts and technologies.

There have been striking successes and notable failures. By and large, organizations that have been able to fully leverage the power of information and information technologies (IT) to develop a competitive advantage have dominated their competitive domains. Those that have been slow to recognize the potential for information and information technologies to transform their organizations and processes, or have failed to go far enough and fast enough to change the way they do business, are being acquired by their competitors or swept away.

This chapter focuses upon the lessons that can be drawn from the experiences in the commercial sector.

We begin by first examining the underlying value-creation processes that are central to developing competitive advantage, then the role played by information and information technologies in enabling and enhancing these processes. The chapter concludes with some examples of how successful organizations have become dominant in their competitive domains by employing information-based strategies and translating information superiority to a competitive advantage.

Some have argued that insights from other domains, such as those we will be drawing from the commercial sector, are not really relevant to military organizations because business is not warfare.[12] It is true that business is not warfare. Myth 7 clearly addresses the inappropriateness of attempting the wholesale transfer of experience from the business domain to the domain of warfare. But to dismiss a potentially rich source of hypotheses for us to examine is as foolish as it is unnecessary. While caution is the watch word, there is a good argument to be made that the basic dynamics of the value-creation process are domain independent. Further, there are significant insights that can be gained from the experiences of dominant competitors who have successfully exploited information technology to create competitive advantage. We see the lessons learned in the commercial sector not as gospel to be blindly followed, but as inputs to our concepts, development, and experimentation processes.

History supports the view that valuable insights have relevance across disparate domains. A fundamental lesson that has emerged from multiple domains, including business and warfare, is that the power of a new technology cannot be fully exploited to create competitive advantage without the simultaneous coevolution of organization and process. This lesson has been learned by those who have explored how militaries have exploited advances in warfighting technologies, such as the long bow, the rifled barrel, the machine gun, the tank, the airplane, radar, and telecommunications. Each of these technologies changed the complexion of warfare. Some of these technologies (airplane, radar, and telecommunications) also had significant commercial applications. In both military and commercial applications, it can be seen in retrospect that effective exploitation of these technologies required the coevolution of organization and doctrine. Thus, technologies have not only migrated from warfare to other domains, but from other domains to warfare. The lessons generated in the initial domain of application have proven useful to those in other domains.

The predominant market for information technology today is the commercial sector. Presently, the defense sector represents a relatively small fraction of the $600-billion-plus information technology market (the percentage varies between 1- and 10-percent-plus of the total market for computing and terrestrial communications, but is much higher for some segments, such as communications satellites).[13] Consequently, the commercial sector is the competitive space with the preponderance of case studies that address the coevolution of organization, process, and information technology in creating competitive advantage. The trajectory of innovation associated with creating competitive advantage in the commercial sector is protrayed in Figure 1, Coevolution and the Shift to Network-Centric Operations. This

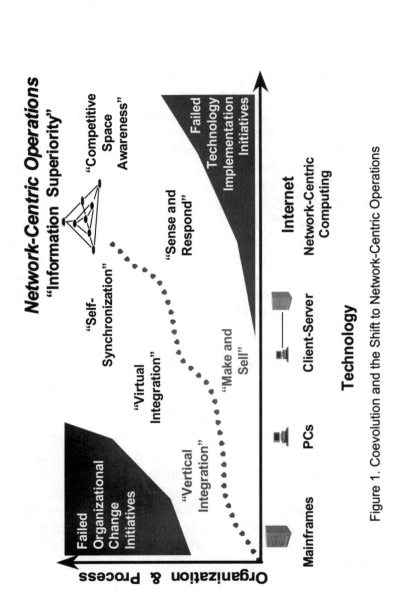

Figure 1. Coevolution and the Shift to Network-Centric Operations

figure highlights the imperative to simultaneously pursue the changes in organization, process, and technology highlighted in the case studies that follow, and to avoid change efforts that focus on only a single dimension of the solution space. The insights that we can gain from the commercial sector can help make DoD a preeminent Information Age organization.

Value Creation

Creation of value is at the heart of creating competitive advantage. As introduced by Michael Porter, the value chain describes the links or processes that transform inputs and/or raw materials into value in the form of products.[14] The value chain concept postulates that competitive advantage can be better understood and hence improved by breaking down the value-creation process depicted in Figure 2 into its constituent parts so that the contribution of each activity to the firm can be assessed. The primary value-creating activities include operations and production, marketing, sales and service, and logistics (both to get the raw material or the inputs to the place where they are processed, assembled, and/or integrated, and get the final product to the customer). Other activities contribute to the value-creation process by playing a supporting role. These support activities include technology development, financial and human resource management, and general infrastructure. The concept of value creation applies equally well to services (referred to as *value shops*, or in the case of brokering or market-creation operations, *value networks.*[15])

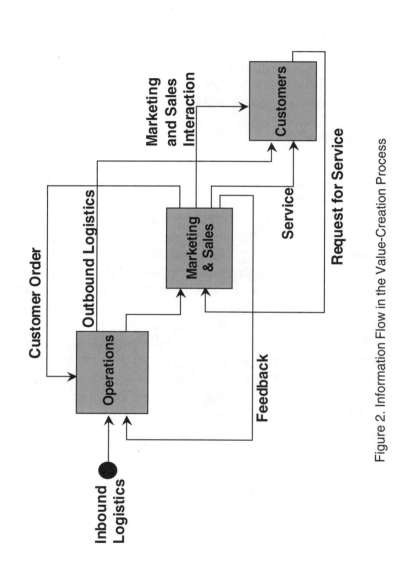

Figure 2. Information Flow in the Value-Creation Process

Figure 3 depicts the key components of the value-creation process. In short, it involves producing an attractive product or service, and making it available in a timely manner at a competitive price.

Increasing competitive advantage requires an increase in the relative value delivered (to customers) vis-à-vis competitors. Value can be enhanced by increasing the attractiveness of a product or service by incorporating the features that customers desire, including the *ilities* (reliability, maintainability, usability, etc.); increasing responsiveness and tempo of operations by reducing time lines (between product innovations and the time from order to delivery); creating concurrent processes; or lowering prices.

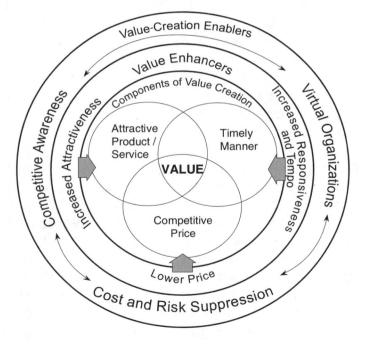

Figure 3. Value-Creation Process

Information and IT are providing the means for innovative companies to create value in ways that were not possible before the advent of the Information Age. The obvious question is: "Where does the value come from, and can it be quantified?"

Insight into the answer to this question is provided by *Metcalfe's Law*.[16] Metcalfe's Law (Figure 4) describes the potential value of a network. It states that as the number of nodes in a network increases *linearly*, the potential "value or "effectiveness" of the network increases *exponentially* as the *square* number of nodes in the network.

The source of potential value is a function of the interactions between the nodes. For every "N" node in a network, there are "N–1" potential interactions between the nodes. Therefore, in a network of "N" nodes, the total number of potential value creating interactions is: $N \times (N-1)$, or N^2-N. For large N, the potential value scales with N^2, or "N squared." (A more in-depth discussion of Metcalfe's Law is provided in Appendix A.)

The existence of the network enables the interactions between nodes to be information intensive. We can observe that information has the dimensions of relevance, accuracy, and timeliness. Therefore, an upper limit in the information domain is reached as information relevance, accuracy, and timeliness approach 100 percent. Of course, organizations may not be able to achieve these 100-percent conditions. Consequently, the objective in the commercial sector is to approach these upper bounds faster than a competitor. Figure 5 portrays a superior information

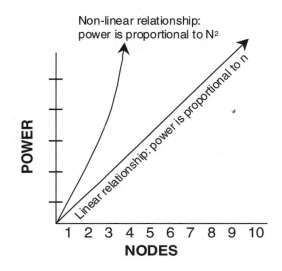

Each node in a network of "N" nodes is capable of initiating "N–1" interactions

Total number of potential interactions between nodes in the network
is:
$N \times (N-1)$ or $N^2 - N$

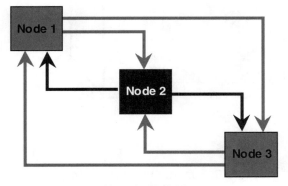

Network with N=3 has

$3 \times 2 = 6$ Potential Information Interactions

Figure 4. Metcalfe's Law

position relative to a competitor in the information domain. The objective is to leverage this superior information position to create and maintain a competitive advantage.

Information Superiority is a state that is achieved when a competitive advantage is derived from the ability to exploit a superior information position.

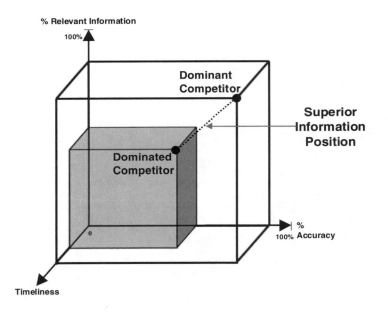

Figure 5. Superior Information Position

The mechanism for creating and exploiting information superiority is a function of the dynamics of competition in a domain of competition. Across broad sectors of the economy, dominant competitors such as Dell Computer Corporation and Cisco Systems (information technology), Federal Express and American Airlines (transportation), Charles Schwab, Deutsche Morgan Grenfell, and Capital One (financial services), and Wal-Mart and Amazon.com (retailing) are successfully employing information-based strategies to create a competitive advantage in their respective domains. Across these domains a number of fundamental themes and concepts have emerged that have coalesced to enable the Network-Centric Enterprise. A Network-Centric Enterprise is characterized by an information-based strategy for creating and exploiting information superiority. The elements of this strategy are depicted in Figure 6.

It all begins with the infostructure ("the entry fee"), which in turn enables the processes that create vastly improved competitive space awareness and share this awareness through the enterprise. This in turn enables a set of processes for exploiting this awareness that results in an improved "bottom line." The remainder of this section explores the nature of the Network-Centric Enterprise.

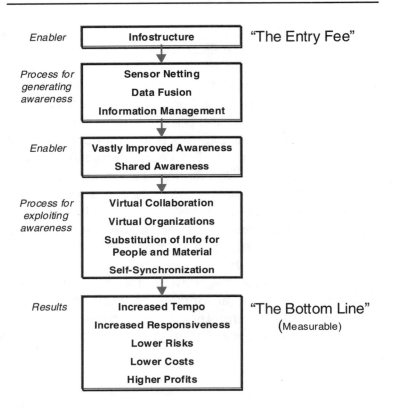

Figure 6. The Network-Centric Enterprise

Competitive Awareness

The ability of a competitive ecosystem to generate and exploit competitive awareness (an awareness of one's competitive domain or competitive space) has emerged as a key enabler of effective decision making and a principle component of competitive advantage in multiple sectors of the economy. As is evident from the case studies discussed later in this chapter, dominant competitors have demonstrated the ability to generate high levels of awareness of what is going on in their respective enterprises and extended business ecosystems. This high level of awareness has been key to both developing strategy and improving effectiveness at the operational level.

Awareness of one's customers, competitors, and the environment is essential to allow organizations to better understand what the characteristics or attributes of their products or services are or need to be to maximize value. Awareness of customer needs also contributes to improved production, capacity, and logistics planning that, in turn, can improve product availability and reduce business risk. For example, decisions often have to be made on how to allocate finite resources against competing needs.

Consider the decisions that need to be made in outbound logistics when demand for product temporarily exceeds supply. From a purely logistical perspective, it would be hard to fault the logic of filling orders on a first-come, first-serve basis. Although this decision logic might be the easiest for logisticians to implement, it could be far from optimal from an enterprise perspective.

To maximize the return for the enterprise, multiple perspectives and factors have to be considered. The history of customer relationships and urgency of customer needs clearly merit consideration. The net profitability of particular customers is a key factor that may influence allocations. Similarly, accounts receivable is likely to place a priority on credit history. The shipping department is likely to be focused on immediate, already scheduled destinations.[17]

The ability of an enterprise to share information across functional areas can enable resource allocation decisions to be made that maximize value from an overall enterprise perspective rather than a purely functional perspective.

Increased awareness of emerging technology will also contribute to leveraging technology to make all of the activities in the value chain more effective and efficient, thus reducing costs and risks. Finally, awareness of the future contributes to the ability to adapt value-creation processes over time to maintain and increase value.

Virtual Organizations

Virtual organizations bring the necessary people and processes together to accomplish a particular task. When the task is over, these resources can be released for other tasks. Virtual organizations, enabled by networking, allow enterprises to take advantage of the potential gains in productivity that are associated with virtual collaboration, virtual integration, and outsourcing. Since networking makes location less important, the opportunities for collaboration, integration, and outsourcing are increased.

Virtual collaboration enables individuals to collaborate in a virtual domain. These individuals can be geographically dispersed. One of the major payoffs of collaboration is an improved product design process— one that is not only faster and less costly, but also produces better designs. Major design efforts, such as the design of aircraft, ships, or automobiles, have been facilitated by the implementation of collaborative digital design processes.[18] A well-publicized case study is Boeing's success in the design of the 777.[19]

Virtual integration enables companies to operate with others as if they were a single, vertically integrated, company. This enables product or market-specific virtual entities to be formed as required to reduce time lines, reduce costs, and improve responsiveness.

Outsourcing is an approach for focusing an organization on its core activities or competencies by divesting activities that must be done but are not where the organization's expertise or experience lies—in other words, areas where it does not possess a competitive advantage. Many organizations have found that outsourcing some of their activities to companies that specialize in a particular service can achieve economies of scale, keep them current with the latest in concepts and technology, or relieve them of the burden of a non-core function. Increasingly, companies have employed outsourcing to accomplish key supporting functions such as information infrastructure, facilities and logistics management, and legal and accounting services. In some cases, activities that used to be considered primary, such as production, have been outsourced and bought as a commodity or turnkey operation. For example, computer manufacturers Compaq and IBM use Ingram Micro to assemble some of their computers. Another example is provided by Sara Lee, which recently announced that it was going to outsource key aspects of production and focus on marketing and product development.[20]

Virtual organizations reduce time lines and increase the tempo of operations. They do this by turning 8-hour days into 24-hour days, by reducing dead times in processes, and by facilitating concurrent processing. In many sectors, increasing the tempo of operations is the key element in achieving competitive advantage. It contributes to reducing costs as well as differentiating products or services based on responsiveness to customer needs. Successful organizations have been able to increase the tempo of their operations by organizing in a manner that allows them to leverage both available information and available assets.

Additional gains can be realized when some of the *collaborators* are, in fact, automated processes or *expert* systems that can provide both greatly increased functionality and simultaneity, along with significant reductions in task processing time.

One of the benefits of adopting network-centric operations is the ability to work projects continuously across time zones. For example, IBM is one of the many companies that now develops and tests software across multiple time zones. After a design team in one location finishes a day's work, another software design team in a separate time zone picks up the ball to continue additional development or testing. Sun Microsystems employs a similar approach to provide support to customers worldwide on a 24-by-7 basis. This basis of "following the sun" can provide significant competitive advantage when time-to-market or service responsiveness is a key source of competitive differentiation.

Cost and Risk Suppression

The ability to use information to suppress costs and reduce prices is at the core of numerous information-based strategies. Many of the approaches for accomplishing cost suppression have been discussed previously. They range from very high payoff, such as being able to reduce the amount of scrap generated in building a large aircraft, (e.g., the Boeing 777[21]) to the truly mundane, such as reducing the time and cost of processing travel claims. There is also the capability in many situations to reduce the need for travel by exploiting video teleconferencing.

A key theme of cost suppression, of which the Boeing 777 is but one example, is the ability to substitute information for inventory. The capability to effectively accomplish this can have a truly significant impact on competitive advantage. As will be evident from the examples that follow, the ability of Wal-Mart and Dell Computer to substitute information for inventory is key to their achieving a competitive advantage.

Risk translates directly into increased costs and/or reduced value. Hence, the reduction of risk and its proper management are an inherent part of value creation. Information (competitive awareness) is, of course, a key to risk suppression.

For example, Capital One, a leading provider of consumer credit, employs very sophisticated analytic techniques to manage operational risk in several ways. First, they employ powerful analytic tools to identify those customers which are likely to have the lowest rates of defaults on their credit card balances. Second, they then exploit this information to focus their marketing efforts on these customers. Third, they employ equally sophisticated tools to align credit card limits with estimates of income and exposure to minimize losses in the event that a customer defaults on loan amounts. The net result of the combination of these approaches is an information-based strategy for managing operational risk that provides significant competitive advantage.[22]

As will be evident from the Dell Computer Corporation example, Dell's ability to substitute information for inventory not only reduces the cost of goods sold, it also significantly reduces two of the primary sources of operational risk: excess parts inventory and excess inventory of finished products.

The examples that follow all serve to illustrate how organizations in the commercial sector are achieving dominant competitive positions that are enabled by information superiority. The first example shows how manufacturing can become precision manufacturing. The second example looks at the transformation of logistics into focused logistics, while the third looks at an example of precision retailing. The final example looks at a case where the *product* is, in and of itself, unique to the Information Age.

Precision Manufacturing

Dell Computer Corporation provides an example of how information can be used to create a competitive advantage in a value chain. Dell Computer Corporation is the world's leading direct computer systems company, with revenues of $18.2 billion for the fiscal year ending February 1, 1999 (up from $12.3 billion for the previous fiscal year, a 48 percent increase). Central to Dell's strategy for creating value is its direct sales model, which offers in-person relationships with corporate and institutional customers; telephone and Internet purchasing; phone and on-line technical support; and next-day, on-site product service.[23]

This approach enables Dell to *"sense and respond"* to producing products only when there is real demand.[24] As a result, Dell has developed a significant competitive advantage over the *"make and sell"* strategies of their competitors. Dell forges strong direct relationships with customers, which among other things allows it to more precisely *sense* the types and kinds of product attributes that are important to various segments of its customer base. This translates into being able to design more attractive products. Equally important, the direct model enables rapid *response* to customer demand while simultaneously reducing operational risk as well as the cost of the end product.

The rapid pace of innovation in the information technology sector provides both risks and opportunities. Two of the primary sources of operational risk are large inventories in the form of excess finished product and obsolete or high priced components (e.g., CPUs, RAM, hard drives, batteries). In some cases, the need to write off excess product and parts inventory has erased an entire quarter's profits.[25] By producing only systems that customers have ordered, Dell minimizes the risk associated with product inventory. Dell reduces risk further by operating with reduced levels of component inventory, which are as small as 11 days for some components. This provides Dell with the capability to respond more quickly than competitors (who in some cases operate with levels of inventory that are over five times larger) when new component technology becomes available, or when prices for existing component technology drop.

Minimizing operational risk in this fashion requires a shift in focus from how much inventory there is to how fast the inventory is moving. Dell manages the *velocity of inventory* by using a constant flow of information to drive operating practices, from performance measures to how they work with suppliers. Dell describes its relationship with its suppliers by using the term *virtual integration*. Virtual integration requires an intensive real-time sharing of information between Dell, its customers, and its suppliers. The ability to share information in near real time among all relevant elements of the ecosystem enables Dell to *substitute information for inventory* and to simultaneously increase flexibility and responsiveness. The near real-time sharing of information within the enterprise provides decision makers with a common operational picture that helps facilitate self-synchronization as well as increase the tempo and responsiveness of operations.

Focused Logistics

In the transportation sector, traditional organizations are entirely focused on the basic service of moving objects from one place to another. In the Information Age, information in the form of in-transit visibility has been added to the *product* to transform logistics into focused logistics. For many customers, this information component of the transportation service often makes or breaks their ability to succeed.

In rail-based shipping, companies such as Union Pacific and CSX now deliver transportation services by combining a primary rail network with a supporting information network. Similarly, shipping companies such as Federal Express and United Parcel Service now employ a primary hub and spoke architecture supported by an information network. The supporting information networks employed by these companies integrate both sensing and transaction capabilities. The sensing capabilities employ networked sensors to generate near real-time awareness on the status and locations of 100 percent of their shipments.[26] In the case of railroads, this translates to thousands of boxcars daily, and in the case of Federal Express and United Parcel Service, daily shipping volume is measured in millions of packages. The ability to generate a high level of awareness has been key to helping these companies identify sources of operational problems and significantly improve their operational performance.[27] Furthermore, the deployment of network enabled transaction capabilities provides customers with operational capabilities for performing on-line transactions (such as placing an order for transportation services, or modifying a transportation request) as well as providing in-transit visibility, in near real time. Thus, these innovative companies differentiate their services in two ways: improved on-time delivery and increased in-transit visibility.

Precision Retailing

In the transaction-intensive retail sector, dominant competitors have used information superiority to create a competitive advantage by adding information to retailing to achieve precision retailing. The recognized leader is Wal-Mart. In 1997, Wal-Mart had earnings of $3.334 billion on sales of $113.42 billion.[28] These sales were generated by a worldwide operation consisting of over 3,000 stores supported by over 1,800 suppliers. Part of Wal-Mart's superior competitive position results from its ability to significantly reduce its distribution costs, which some have estimated to be less than 3 percent of sales, versus 4½ to 5 percent for the competition.[29] In a sector where margins are razor thin, the relationship between these reduced distribution costs and Wal-Mart's profitability is clear. Furthermore in this light, Wal-Mart's ability to reduce inventory in 1997 by over $1 billion can be seen as a truly significant accomplishment.

The competitive advantage that enables this cost suppression emerged when Wal-Mart realized that it could not cost effectively synchronize supply and demand from the top down. Wal-Mart has moved from a traditional retailer to a *precision retailer* by achieving information superiority in its domain. Implementing this strategy required the coevolution of organization and process and, as part of the entry fee, an information infrastructure consisting of a sensory capability and semi-automated transaction capabilities. Wal-Mart employs this *infostructure* to generate a high level of competitive awareness in its retail ecosystem and exploits this awareness to create value.

The sensors include point of sales scanners that collect information on the 90 million (on average) transactions that take place each week.[30] Sharing this information with suppliers in near real time enables suppliers to optimally control production and distribution, as well as manage their individual supply chains. In the words of Jack Welch, the CEO of General Electric:

> *When Wal-Mart sells a [light]bulb on the register, it goes to my factory instantly—I [General Electric] make the bulb for the one they just sold. The enterprise system is now totally compressed with information.*[31]

This degree of self-synchronization emerged from the coevolution of organization and process. Originally, Wal-Mart had a central purchasing department. But when the decision was made to share information directly with suppliers, the need for this part of the organization went away. Costs were reduced and performance increased.

A high level of awareness is generated at each Wal-Mart store by fusing real-time information with historical and environmental information. To accomplish this, all transaction information is stored in a large data warehouse (24-plus terabytes) where it is analyzed with sophisticated data mining algorithms to extract trend data (e.g., seasonal trends, market basket trends).[32] This is then combined with real-time transaction information to develop a high degree of localized awareness within each Wal-Mart store. For example, sales statistics for each 100,000-plus products are generated on a store-by-store basis, permitting department managers in each Wal-Mart store (there are 36 departments in the typical Wal-Mart store) to compare daily sales figures with historic sales figures from the previous day, the previous week, and the same periods the previous year. In addition, each department manager is able to determine in real time existing inventory levels, the amount of product in transit (in-transit visibility), and inventory levels at neighboring Wal-Mart stores. This very high level of awareness enables local section managers to identify opportunities in near real time and take appropriate action to increase sales and revenues. Actions include repricing items to react to local competitors' pricing moves or prominently displaying items that are experiencing increased volume or those that are generating high margins.

Superior competitive awareness enables Wal-Mart to suppress costs, increase sales, and improve net earnings.

The Network Is the Market

In the financial services sector, where information is the life-blood of markets, the emergence of real-time awareness and real-time transaction capabilities is changing the dynamics of competition. Companies such as Charles Schwab and E*Trade have introduced capabilities for real-time on-line stock trading that create value by providing customers with new trading capabilities and reduced costs. These companies are using information and information technologies to achieve time compression and cost suppression. Time compression is enabled by capabilities that provide near real-time price awareness and enable near real-time transactions. Cost suppression is achieved in large measure by replacing the traditional approach of dealing directly with a broker via telephone or in person with more direct digital access. Employing a strategy based upon information superiority has enabled Schwab to emerge as the leading provider of on-line trading services with a market capitalization that recently exceeded that of Merrill Lynch.[33]

Similar value creation trends have emerged in the worldwide multitrillion dollar market for interest-bearing U.S. Government securities. In this market, the introduction of the *Autobahn* automated trading service by Deutsche Morgan Grenfell, Inc. (DMG) is fundamentally changing the dynamics of competition by creating a new trading ecosystem where *The Network is the Market*[SM].

In the existing trader-centric ecosystem, the trader holds important information, placing him in a position of power. Customers potentially work with multiple traders to initiate and complete a transaction. The transaction is a three-step process involving generation of price awareness, selection of a trader, and execution of a transaction. Transaction timelines are dominated by access timelines, and service asymmetries emerge between large and small customers. For large customers, a transaction takes 30 to 90 seconds or so under ideal conditions. For small customers, a transaction can take an order of magnitude longer. When major market movements take place, competition based on time emerges as the dominant competitive dynamic and service asymmetries are amplified. When trading volumes are extremely large, traders can exploit their position of power by raising the minimum amount for trades.[34][35] With *Autobahn*, DMG eliminates asymmetry with information superiority. The shift to network-centric operations enables DMG to provide all customers with 100 percent competitive space awareness in real time. This awareness is in the form of bid and ask prices for the 200-plus notes and bonds of varying yields and maturities that make up the market. Price information is broadcast to all approved customers, large and small, over the Bloomberg Financial Services Network. Customers can exploit this real-time awareness to initiate and complete a transaction in 2 seconds 95 percent of the time. In making the shift to network-centric operations, DMG has employed an operational architecture with three primary components:

1) a sensing capability which collects and fuses public domain information on the market;
2) a transaction capability, which contains several analytic engines which essentially perform the function of command and control, enabling the very high speed 2-second transaction timelines; and
3) an information infrastructure in the form of the Bloomberg Financial Services Network.

DMG has identified the competitive attributes required to operate more effectively in its competitive space, and it has also changed its business to reflect the value of those competitive attributes. Because of that, it is rapidly capturing market share and other firms, under intense competitive pressure, are attempting to coevolve their organizations and processes.[36]

Lessons and Insights

Integrating across the experiences of the firms that have emerged as dominant in their competitive domains, the following core themes are revealed.

1) Information technologies enable firms to create a high level of competitive awareness within their organizations and extended enterprises.
2) Networking is enabling the creation of new types of information-based relationships with and among organizations that are able to leverage increased competitive awareness.
3) Time is being compressed and, as a result, the tempo of operations is being increased.
4) The cumulative impact of better information, better distribution, and new organizational behavior provides firms with the capability to create superior value propositions for their customers and dominate their competitive space.

As we will see in the chapters that follow, these emerging themes have direct application across the spectrum of military operations. If applied wisely, they will transform DoD into an Information Age Organization that will continue to dominate its competitive domain.

Implications for Military Operations

In the last section we have seen how the Information Age is affecting organizations engaged in commercial activities, noting that these changes are driven by changes in the environments in which they operate and the capabilities they have at their disposal. These developments in the private sector are a harbinger of change and provide us with an opportunity to anticipate what factors have the potential to profoundly affect military organizations and operations. Information Age organizations achieve domination of their ecosystems by developing and exploiting information superiority. This section defines the concept of information superiority in military operations and examines the changes in the operating environment, or competitive space of military organizations, and the emerging capabilities that affect our ability to understand and influence this competitive space.

Specifically, we will look at the changed nature of our mission(s), the battlespace in which we operate, our adversaries' capabilities, our ability to sense and understand the battlespace, the capability of the weapons at our disposal, and—perhaps most important of all—our ability to command and control.

Information Superiority

JV2010 parallels the changes that are taking place in pioneering commercial organizations that are being transformed into Network-Centric Enterprises. JV2010 asserts that the operational concepts of dominant maneuver, precision engagement, full-dimensional protection, and focused logistics will be enabled by information superiority. The desired end-state is full-spectrum dominance. Information superiority, as currently defined in Joint Pub 3-13 below, addresses only the achievement of a superior information position.

> *The ability to collect, process, and disseminate an uninterrupted flow of information while exploiting and/or denying an adversary's ability to do the same.*
>
> —Joint Pub 3-13

In drawing a parallel from our discussion of the commercial sector, we view *Information Superiority* in military operations as a state that is achieved when competitive advantage (e.g., full-spectrum dominance) is derived from the ability to exploit a superior information position. In military operations this superior information position is, in part, gained from information operations that protect our ability to collect, process, and disseminate an uninterrupted flow of information while exploiting and/or denying an adversary's ability to do the same.

As in the commercial sector, information has the dimensions of relevance, accuracy, and timeliness. And as in the commercial sector, the upper limit in the information domain is reached as information relevance, accuracy, and timeliness approach 100 percent. Of course, as in the commercial sector, we may never be able to approach these limits. Figure 7 portrays a superior information position relative to a competitor in military operations. The desired effect of offensive information operations is to drive one or more components of the competitor's information "volume" towards the origin. The desired effect of defensive information operations is to keep our information "volume" from being compressed.

Figure 8 depicts the achievement of full-spectrum dominance resulting from generating and exploiting a superior information position.

Clearly, information superiority is a comparative or relative concept. Furthermore, its value is clearly derived from the military outcomes it can enable. In this sense, it is analogous to air superiority or sea control. These capabilities are not valued for themselves, but for making extended offensive and defensive actions more effective.[37] Achieving information superiority increases the speed of command preempting adversary options, creates new options, and improves the effectiveness of selected options. This promises to bring operations to a successful conclusion more rapidly at a lower cost. The result is an ability to increase the tempo of operations and to preempt or blunt adversary initiatives and options. Information superiority is generated and exploited by adopting the network-centric concepts, pioneered in the commercial sector, that allow organizations to achieve shared awareness and self-synchronization. The bottom line for value creation in military operations involves the detection,

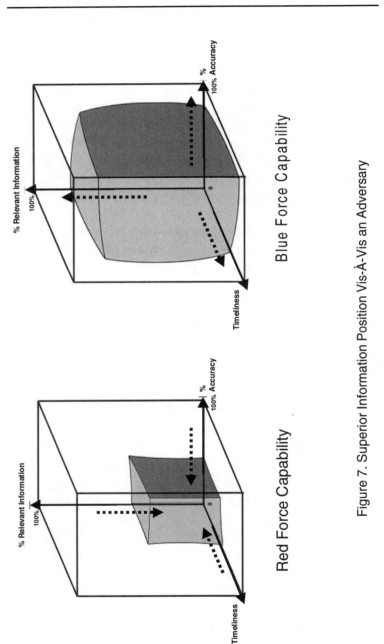

Figure 7. Superior Information Position Vis-À-Vis an Adversary

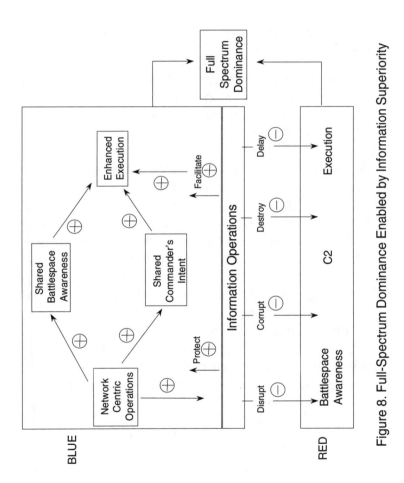

Figure 8. Full-Spectrum Dominance Enabled by Information Superiority

identification, and disposal of the most important targets at any given time. The biggest challenge lies in fleeting targets, those that are mobile and whose value is time sensitive.

What's Different about the Mission Space and the Battlespace

The mission space relevant to U.S. national security is expanding and becoming more complex. The United States, as the only superpower, has a key role to play in the post-Cold War era. Our roles and responsibilities are somewhat different from those we had in a bipolar world. Several important differences affecting military organizations and operations have already manifested themselves. The first is the increasing importance of operations other than war (OOTW) in which military organizations are being tasked to do a wide variety of non-traditional missions, from humanitarian relief to peace enforcement.[38] Second, while these differences stem from geopolitical considerations, other changes in the mission space are driven by technology. Third is the emergence of the possibility of an entirely new form of warfare, Information Warfare, or perhaps more generically, Infrastructure Warfare. Finally, asymmetrical forms of warfare have become significantly more potent with the increased lethality and accessibility of weapons of mass destruction (WMD).

Each of these changes has important implications for the types of capabilities we need and the constraints and stresses that are placed upon us. The undertaking of a wide variety of OOTW missions requires access to new organizations and information. We will need to work closely with non-government organizations (NGOs) and private voluntary organizations (PVOs), associations that have relationships and agendas that often place constraints on their interactions with military organizations, and hence create a great deal of stress.[39] The need to operate effectively as part of a coalition requires some modifications to our most cherished notions about command and control, particularly the principle of the unity of command[40] and the ability to exchange information with others. Information operations, in its cyberwar form, has the potential to totally redefine the nature of warfare,[41] blur the boundaries between civilian and military responsibilities, provide a new set of weapons, and create new vulnerabilities. Information operations is an umbrella term that encompasses a wide variety of offensive and defensive activities. Offensive information operations is the subset of these activities that involves the use of digital weapons against digital targets anywhere in the battlespace. For example, it may be the insertion of a virus in an adversary command and control system or it may be a similar attack on an adversary's critical infrastructure systems (e.g., power, communications, public safety).

All of these changes have profound implications for the measures or indicators of success we use to assess and analyze operations. In some instances the line between war and peace and between friend, foe, and neutral is blurred beyond recognition. Asymmetric warfare presents a unique set of challenges, not the least of which is finding successful strategies for deterrence, detection, and response. Lethal weapons may become of little value in many situations when the political costs of using them far outweigh their effects. Asymmetric warfare involves each side playing by its own set of rules that emphasize their respective strengths, while attempting to exploit an adversary's weakness. It is a far cry from the tank-on-tank battles or naval engagements of the past. This makes it very difficult to develop indications and warnings to alert us to someone preparing for war. Rather than working around the clock to produce aircraft, an adversary may be educating computer scientists or recruiting computer hackers.

If we look at these changes as a whole, it is clear that our missions have become far more complex and our challenges and adversaries less predictable. The information we need to sort things out has become, simultaneously, more diverse and more specific. Our measures of merit have also become more varied and complex, and our tool kit needs to be greatly expanded to handle more complex and varied situations. Dealing with this complexity will be a major challenge requiring us to approach problems and tasks somewhat differently.

In one sense, the battlespace of the 21st century will be defined by the mission space, and in another by the very nature of the Information Age. The term battlespace recently replaced battlefield to convey a sense that the mission environment or competitive space encompasses far more than a contiguous physical place. At the risk of oversimplification, the Information Age is changing the battlespace in three fundamental ways. The first involves the expansion of the battlefield as just mentioned. The second is in the nature of combatants in the battlespace, and the third is in its loss of privacy and remoteness. Each of these is discussed below.

While it is true that targets have always ranged from strategic to tactical, and have included the psychological as well as the physical, Information Age target sets will be expanded, and the relative priority of different kinds of targets will change. The expansion of the target sets is driven both by the growth in the variety of missions and in the possibilities created by advances in technology. The nature of OOTW or strategic information operations certainly puts some traditional targets out of bounds while placing more emphasis on others. The employment of information operations in traditional combat involves the use of new weapons against both traditional as well as new targets. For example, we will now have the option of a variety of cyber attacks on a communications router, a database, or a decision aid (to disrupt or degrade an enemy air defense asset), in addition to physical attacks on enemy air defenses. Or we could use both types of attacks in a coordinated manner to achieve the suppression of enemy air defenses. The costs, nature of the effects, lethality, collateral damage, ability to do battle damage assessment, covertness, and adversary and public responses will likely differ not only in our selection of targets, but also in the way they were attacked. This adds a whole new dimension that increases the complexity of a situation and the task of developing a response. Further, even in traditional combat situations with kinetic weapons, the improved range, lethality, and precision will tend to spread out the battlespace.

When these improvements in weapons are combined with improvements in sensors and analysis, concentrated forces will present high-value targets that will become increasingly vulnerable in the Information

Age. Furthermore, while the Information Age is making information available almost anywhere, almost anytime, and at reduced costs, it is not having the same effect on the economics of transportation for personnel and materiel.

Therefore, it will make the movement of information far less costly than the movement of physical things. Thus, the economic dynamics of the Information Age will drive solutions that leave people and machines where they are (a smaller in-theater footprint), and use information to make those in theater more effective—that is, to find ways to put them in the right place more often, and mass effects rather than forces. Only the pointy end of the spear will move on the battlefield of the future. Thus, the battlespace is extended by virtue of the increase in the number and variety of targets of interest and their dispersion.

The nature of the combatants in the battlespace of the future will of course depend upon the mission. Although civilians have been involved as victims and in supporting roles throughout history, they will play an increasingly important role in the battlespaces of the future. Again, this is driven by the nature of the missions that will be undertaken. For example, information operations may be conducted entirely in the civilian sector. OOTW involve both civilian and military organizations as participants.

To succeed in these missions requires that the actions of the military and civilian organizations be coordinated far more closely than they needed to be in traditional combat situations. This puts opposing military and civilian organizations in new juxtapositions. In addition to having new classes of combatants present in the battlespace, their identities will be less clear. Guerrilla warfare and sabotage were examples of this in the past.

One of the greatest challenges we will face will be to ascertain the identity and location of our adversaries in the battlespaces of the future. Terrorists using real or logic bombs could strike from almost anywhere, and the distinction between a foreign threat and a domestic one will become blurred. (When does this become a military vs. a civilian problem?) Even in traditional warfare situations, one can expect that considerable efforts will be made to become stealthy and develop disguises. If what can be seen can be reliably killed, then the response will be to avoid being seen and thus the battlespace will become a place to play hide and seek.[42]

The third characteristic of the battlespace of the future is that it will no longer be private or remote. The Vietnam War was an early example of this. It was fought as much, if not more, in the living rooms of America as in the living jungles of Southeast Asia. More recently we experienced a similar visible "defeat" in Somalia. The battlespace for these operations was no longer confined to the battlefield.[43] The Information Age has changed the access that combatants and non-combatants alike have to information. This is because militaries and national security agencies no longer have exclusive control of real-time information. The commercial availability of quality images, location devices, access to vast stores of information, and high bandwidth circuits provide even the poorest nations or non-state actors with access to information recently available only to superpowers.

CNN and its competitors, combined with the Internet, make this information available to almost any interested person. Commercial satellites provide real-time images that are used to support a wide variety of tasks, including weather forecasting, oil exploration, and environmental analyses. These very same images could provide affordable information for potential adversaries.

The Information Age, by making it possible to collect and disseminate images widely, is seemingly bringing us a modern-day version of the Circus Maximus 24 hours a day, 7 days a week. To know is to get involved, and in a democracy, involvement means public debate. Learning to live with friends and foes alike looking over one's shoulder in real time will be a formidable challenge and can be expected to affect how we approach potential and real threats to national security.

With the glare of the public spotlight on everything, each individual event takes on a potential importance unlike anything in past times. This makes it necessary to rethink how we allocate decisions and how we educate and train our people. With one's adversaries having potentially increased visibility into our deliberations, decision-making processes, preparations, and operations, there is an increased risk of being outflanked or disrupted. In one sense the situation actually becomes more like chess, where everyone gets the same pieces and sees the same battlespace. The winner, of course, is the one who can make the best use of the pieces.

Obviously, we will also do what we can to obscure the board and alter the capabilities of the pieces. But none of this will work unless we can prevent our adversaries from altering the rules of the game to their advantage, so that we have no good moves and no good outcomes.

A major effect of the fishbowl environment of the Information Age is its effect on the amount of time we have to make a decision. Highly placed decision makers around the globe have noted the greatly increased pressures upon them to react quickly to breaking events, often first finding out about these potential crises, not from their traditional sources, but from the news media. It is ironic that the Information Age, which on one hand gives us vastly increased capabilities to collect and process data that make it possible to make better and better decisions more and more quickly, is—with the other hand—reducing the time available to make decisions. Thus, the race is on. We need to either find ways to respond more quickly with quality decisions, or to find ways to extend the time for critical decisions by expediting other parts of the process.

What's Different about Sensors and Actors

Technology will, of course, vastly improve the performance of the sensors and actors we have. Moreover, we will achieve increases in performance while reducing unit costs, increasing the number of sensors and actors we can afford to buy. However significant these advances are, the real payoff will come from four other differences between the sensors and the actors of today and those of the Information Age. The first will involve a transfer of intelligence from the weapons or sensors to an information infrastructure or "infostructure," and a corresponding relocation of complexity from the platform to the network. The technical term for this is the development of *thin clients*—entities with a minimum amount of processing and data storage capability that connect to servers. Of course, the thin clients of tomorrow will have many times the capability that current *thick* clients have today.

The second will involve the decoupling of sensors from weapons platforms, in other words, the end of stove-piping. The third will come from a decoupling of sensors and weapons platforms from actors. The fourth will be the development of new sensors to sense new types of entities and new actors to provide us with novel capabilities to damage our adversaries. Each of these is discussed below.

First, the proper distribution of intelligence among the entities of a system depends upon a number of factors related to the nature of the tasks that need to be accomplished, including the locations of the sources of information, the relative costs and reliability of computing and telecommunications, the costs of the entities themselves, the relative values of different types and levels of intelligence, and security considerations. The economics of smart weapons depend a great deal on where the smarts are located. It will be feasible in the Information Age to make relatively dumb weapons appear smart by embedding dynamic intelligence in an infostructure. The dumb/ smart weapons will only need to know how to obey, not how to determine what needs to be done.

Today's smart weapons have a fairly sophisticated set of capabilities on board. This degree of intelligence enables them to be fired, perhaps to be updated with the latest information, and forgotten, leaving the terminal phase to the smart weapon that engages the target and pursues it if necessary. Dumb/smart weapons only need to be able to navigate to a point in space and time. All other functionality would be incorporated into the infostructure. The advantages of this approach will be discussed later in the section on implications.

The second and third significant changes both involve decoupling. One involves the elimination of stove-pipe sensor weapon pairings. Information Age technologies will provide the means to achieve greater interoperability and alter the micro-economic incentives and practical considerations that often drive us towards point solutions. This is the rough equivalent of moving from producing rifles one-by-one by hand, to manufacturing them with interchangeable parts.

The other involves decoupling sensors and actors from the platforms that carry them today. Platforms serve a multitude of purposes. The Information Age provides us alternative means of achieving some of these for the first time. Among the services the platforms provide are transportation, power, integration, and connectivity to decision makers. But platforms have large footprints and are difficult to make stealthy. In addition, they are very expensive to produce, man, and defend. The economics of platforms and force structure limit the number we can buy and operate. The limited number reduces our flexibility to position them to respond to simultaneous situations and their high value increases their attractiveness as targets.

NCW has the potential to enhance the value of existing platforms by extending the effective ranges of their sensors and weapons. Advances in technology provide the opportunity to move the functionality provided by platforms to either the infostructure, the sensors, or the actor, thus permitting us to decouple functions from traditional platforms.

The fourth change is the need to invent and deploy a host of new sensors and actors:

1) sensors designed to sense new things and maneuver in close to make distinctions among things we cannot now distinguish; and
2) actors designed to achieve new effects while at the same time becoming far more stealthy.

Information operations are the ultimate in stealth. For example, one of the greatest challenges in information operations is simply to know when one is under attack. We are in the process of working on a new class of sensors that could provide this information. These need to be developed if we are to have adequate defenses in this area.

The net result of all of these changes will be the proliferation of lower cost, independent sensors and actors that will contribute to and depend more upon distributed rather than embedded intelligence. How the capabilities of these dispersed entities will be leveraged is the subject of the next section.

Challenges and Opportunities for Command and Control

Command and control is a broad term covering a multitude of activities at all levels of an organization. Folded into this term is everything from inspiring and motivating the individuals in the organization, to setting and conveying a common sense of purpose, to assigning responsibilities, to assessing how well the organization is performing.

Command and control is inherently an iterative decision-making process, as feedback from the battlespace is incorporated into plans and corrective actions. Warfare has always been a challenging domain characterized by the importance of the endeavor, risk to life, sheer magnitude of the effort, and management of uncertainty. Our approaches to command and control have been honed over time to meet these challenges. However, the Information Age-driven changes described in the preceding sections present us with a host of new command and control challenges. In this section we will examine these challenges and catalog the opportunities for improvement.

Military operations are (should be) designed to accomplish a task or solve a problem. As in other human endeavors, often the biggest problem is recognizing that there is a problem and knowing the nature of the problem. The art of military problem formulation often involves recognizing and making distinctions between tactical and strategic problems and putting them into perspective (an overall context). The development of a campaign is the formulation of a series of interrelated problems. The campaign model for a military operation is the essence of long-range or strategic planning.

Our current approach to developing a military campaign plan is predicated upon a fairly well understood set of relationships among events that take time to unfold. Thus, the plan can be decomposed into a series of steps, each one building in a linear fashion on the preceding steps. Our ability to deal with something as complex as a military campaign depends upon our ability to break it down into these manageable pieces. We can do so because of our ability to separate events in time and space. Organizationally, we deal at three levels—the strategic, operational, and tactical. Geographically, we deal with sectors or theaters. Functionally, we usually deal with specific jobs or tasks in a sequential manner (e.g., first we do suppression of enemy air defenses and achieve air superiority, then we attack other targets). The battlespace is thus segmented, and we can deal with smaller isolated problems, tasks, or battles.

The nature of Information Age Warfare makes it more and more difficult to operate in this reductivist fashion. Technology has compressed the space and time continuum, and political realities have collapsed the clear separations among the strategic, operational, and tactical levels by introducing more dynamic rules of engagement. The new *Circus Maximus* introduces a dose of chaos, and the Wired World makes the process nonlinear. We will find it necessary to manage larger and larger pieces, and do it more and more quickly in situations that are unlike those of former ages.

At the same time we will need to integrate orders of magnitude more sources of information provided by new armies of sensors to develop, in one way or another, a coherent picture of the battlespace, and fashion our responses in a distributed environment. This is the basic nature of the command and control challenge of the Information Age. It is not surprising that some who are beginning to understand the nature of the daunting challenge are not eager to take it on and would like the past to hold on for a bit longer. This approach ignores both the immediacy of the challenge and the potential payoff.

All of this challenges our most basic assumptions about command and control and the doctrine developed for a different time and a different problem. One of the most enduring lessons derived from the history of warfare is the degree to which fog and friction permeate the battlespace. The fog of battle is about the uncertainty associated with what is going on, while the friction of war is about the difficulty in translating the commander's intent into actions. Much of the fog of war, or what is referred to today as a lack of battlespace awareness, has resulted in our inability to tap into our collective knowledge, or the ability to assemble existing information, reconcile differences, and construct a common picture. There needs to be equal emphasis placed upon developing a current awareness of both friendly and enemy dispositions and capabilities, and in many cases, there needs to be increased emphasis on neutrals. Traditionally, the responsibilities for each of these interrelated pieces of battlespace awareness have been parsed to different organizations, resulting in significant barriers to pulling together a complete picture. The rest of the problem is a lack of coverage resulting from limited-range sensors and their ability to discriminate.

The friction of war derives from a variant of Murphy's Law, exacerbated by the difficulty in clearly communicating information to people and resulting differences of perception. Dealing with a battlespace permeated with fog and needing to develop plans that must survive the worst of Murphy have been preeminent commander's challenges since the dawn of warfare. Command and control, as we know it, was developed to meet this challenge. Dealing with the fog and friction of war places the relative emphasis on:

1) not making a big mistake;
2) not harming one's own;
3) achieving a semblance of cohesion;
4) maximizing effectiveness; and
5) achieving economies of force.[44]

Deliberate planning, massing of forces, use of reserves, rigid doctrine, restricted information flows, and emphasis on unity of command are among the legacy of centuries of dealing with the fog and friction of war.

While the Information Age will not eliminate the fog and friction of war, it will surely significantly reduce it, or at the very least change the nature of the uncertainties. We need to rethink the concepts and practices that were born out of a different reality. We need to begin by looking at the way we currently formulate military problems and the nature of the solutions we favor. Individuals tend to formulate problems based upon their expertise and experience.

In other words, they tend to think in the box. Simply put, the Information Age is changing the box in a number of dimensions. In its most basic form, the problem box consists of an objective function (mission objectives), a set of options (courses of actions, approaches, tools), and states (enemy actions, circumstances, etc.). We have noted earlier that the Information Age has altered mission objectives, limited some earlier options, provided new options, altered the nature of the states considered through changing circumstances, and provided our potential adversaries with new capabilities.

The Information Age has also had an effect on how we solve problems and implement solutions. Solving a problem boils down to making a decision or series of decisions (selecting an alternative). In military operations, formulating and making command decisions are part of a well-understood planning process, and the implementation of these decisions is part of a well-oiled execution process.

The Information Age has changed the way we reach decisions, allocate decision responsibilities within the organization, develop options and evaluate them, and the manner in which we choose among them. This has obvious implications in how we design systems and train people. The Information Age has created an environment where collaborative decision making can be employed to increase combat power, partly because of the emergence of coalition operations, partly because of the distribution of awareness and knowledge in the battlespace, and partly because of the compression of decision timelines. This alone would be challenging enough, but the Information Age has also transformed the problem of warfare from a series of static events to a more continuous one by greatly increasing the operating tempo of events. The result is the need for greater integration between the heretofore separate planning and execution processes, requiring more timely interactions between the two, and portents an ultimate merging of these two processes into a seamless form of command and control.

In the past the command and control process has been characterized by an iterative sequential series of steps. Various representations of this form all include sensing, fusing, understanding, deciding, conveying the decisions, and acting (execution). The cycle starts again with battlespace damage assessment (BDA).

Three such models of the command and control process are:

1) the observation, orientation, decision, action (OODA) cycle attributed to former Air Force Colonel John Boyd;
2) a model consisting of sense, process, compare, decide, and act steps, developed by Dr. Joel S. Lawson;[45]
3) the headquarters effectiveness assessment tool (HEAT) process, consisting of monitor, understand, develop alternative actions, predict, decide, and direct steps, developed by Dr. Richard E. Hayes and others at Defense Systems, Inc., in 1984.[46]

These decision or command and control loops exist at various echelons and subordinate loops are embedded accordingly. Planning is a form of decision making that exists at a headquarters level. When viewed over time, the activities at the different echelons take place sequentially, with one level executing the existing plan while another is developing the new plan. This process has evolved to the point where planning and execution are distinct activities. Efforts to speed up the process so that more responsive plans can be developed are fast approaching the laws of diminishing returns (their natural limits).

In fact the entire loop concept for command and control is becoming outdated and needs to be replaced with a new concept of command and control—one that recognizes the need to treat different types of decisions differently and recognizes a merging of the now separate planning and execution processes (sometimes called dynamic planning).

Command and control practices have evolved over time as missions and capabilities have changed. Different military establishments have taken different approaches to command and control to fit the qualities and characteristics of their organizations.[47]

Often new command and control concepts arise out of a desire to leverage new capability that provides increased information. An illustration of this is the emergence of the concept of "Command by Negation" within the U.S. Navy. In June of 1972, the U.S. Navy introduced the F-14A into the Fleet as a replacement for the F-4 as its front line Fleet air defense fighter. The F-14A had a number of significant performance advantages over the F-4, one of which was its ability to generate a superior level of onboard situational awareness. This superior awareness was generated by the AWG-9 radar, which provided the F-14A crew with an actual target video symbol, as opposed to raw radar returns provided by the AWG-10 radar deployed on F-4s.

This superior situational awareness remained unexploited for over 6 years, as the Fleet Air Defense Mission continued to use the same command and control doctrine employed with the F-4s. This doctrine called for fighters to be directed to targets by controllers operating in E-2s and Ship Combat Information Centers with positive control enforced when available.

The potential for F-14As to generate increased combat power became apparent in 1978 during exercise *Beacon South*. During this exercise, Royal Australian Air Force pilots, employing aggressive maneuvers designed to make tracking difficult, were able to penetrate the battle group's air defenses with their F-111s. During the exercise, U.S. Navy pilots flying F-14As had the F-111s in track, but were directed away from the F-111s by a ship-based CIC controller to what turned out to be nonexistent targets. As a result of the lessons learned from this exercise, the command and control doctrine of "Vector Logic" was approved for use in the 7th Fleet. The following year, the command and control doctrine of "Command by Negation" was approved for Fleet-wide use. Finally, this doctrine provided F-14A crews with a rule set that enabled them to exploit their superior onboard situational awareness to engage targets at will unless otherwise directed by operational commanders.[48]

The above example illustrated a change in doctrine in order to take advantage of increased battlespace awareness. Sometimes, a change in the very structure of an organization is necessary in order to exploit increased awareness. The emphasis on hierarchy and other legacy concepts and practices that were needed to accommodate the fog and friction of war have remained mainstays of command and control (e.g., unity of command and coupling information flow to the command hierarchy). One basic driver of hierarchy is span of control. Traditionally, the rule of thumb for an acceptable span of control has been "5, plus or minus 2." This was based on how many relationships an individual could effectively manage. This relatively small span of control has resulted in large organizations having many levels, creating a huge middle management. Large organizations have become ponderous and sluggish by today's Information Age standards. Information flow has slowed and is reduced to a trickle of its potential. Clearly this is not acceptable in the Information Age. To break this mold we need to effectively increase the span of control. Fortunately, the Information Age gives us the tools to do so.

The characteristics of the Information Age and the nature of the missions we will undertake in the 21st century make it important that we reexamine these basic tenets. We must realize that they are not immutable laws of nature, but solutions to problems that have been refined over the years. We have seen from the lessons of recent coalition operations[49] that unity of command may be infeasible, and one may need to strive instead for unity of effort. We have seen from the lessons of fledgling Information Age organizations that restricting information flow to the hierarchy is a losing strategy.[50] We are beginning to realize that our advances in technology promise to reduce the fog and friction of war to the point where it no longer makes sense to devote scarce resources to restrict information to the extent we have in the past. Our freedom to search for a more appropriate way to approach command and control in the Information Age is our greatest opportunity. We cannot afford to let this opportunity slip through our fingers, for our potential adversaries will most certainly not. The reason that our competitors cannot be counted on to ignore this opportunity is that it offers a non-capital intensive way to create an effective asymmetric capability, and many of these competitors are neither hampered by huge investments in legacy systems, nor the tyranny of past successes.

Implications for Future Command and Control

Starting with a clean sheet of paper, how would we describe the requirements for future command and control, and what implications do these requirements have for our approach to shaping and managing the battlespace? It should be noted that the task has been cast as managing the battlespace, not just managing our assets or forces. (The use of the term management here does not imply control, but should be read broadly enough to include influence.)

We can start by identifying what needs to be managed, noting that attention needs to be focused on the interactions among entities. First, of course, are our sensors and actors. Second is the supporting infostructure. Third, and arguably the most important focus of command and control, is the need to manage battlespace information (information should not be confused with the systems that process and carry this information, a part of our infostructure). Fourth, are perceptions, including those of our own, our coalition partners, neutrals, and adversaries. The importance, indeed the centrality, of information is what distinguishes warfare in the Information Age from warfare in previous times. This is not to deny that information has always been important in warfare, but argues that the nature and amount of information available, and our improved ability to distribute it, will have a profound impact on the way warfare is conducted. This is discussed in detail in the next section.

We will need to make investments in all of the elements that comprise a mission capability package. This is to ensure that we have:

1) an organization and doctrine that are compatible with the concept of operations;
2) the information flows necessary to carry them out;
3) properly educated and trained personnel; and
4) a set of systems that are able to exchange and utilize the available information.

As we move to a thin client architecture, the unit costs of our sensors and actors will be reduced. These savings in unit costs will enable us to buy larger quantities of sensors and actors and to invest in the infostructure we need to support them by increasing our ability to fuse information and disseminate it intelligently.

Our next considerations are the different kinds of battlespaces we expect to encounter. Each will be driven by the characteristics of the mission, and each will have its own set of requirements that will make it necessary to tailor not only our force packages, but also our approach to command and control. One size or approach to command and control will not fit all situations. Thus, while the basic function or objective of command and control remains the same (that is, to make the most of the situation and the resources at hand), how this is accomplished (the command and control approach) will differ significantly from situation to situation. To make matters more challenging, significant differences will exist within a single battlespace, and hence there may need to be different approaches to command and control that coexist in harmony.

Finally, we need to consider the impact of the Information Age on the above as it relates to the job of command and control. The Information Age will not only have a dramatic effect on reducing the fog and friction of war, but will also permit us to consider and employ force with greater precision and granularity.

Currently the public's perception of this ability appears to be well beyond our actual abilities, which causes expectations to be somewhat unrealistic. This in turn puts considerable pressure on how we respond. The military will be judged not only by whether or not a mission was accomplished, but also whether or not it accomplished the mission with an appropriate level of force, or the minimum level to achieve the effect. Traditional military operations, conceived and conducted under the doctrine of overwhelming force, may prove to have adverse political consequences.

Thus, while our tool kit will be augmented by Information Age capabilities, our ability to use them all effectively remains unrealized. To take full advantage of these new precise tools requires that we not only achieve levels of battlespace awareness significantly higher than we have today, but also be able to deploy these tools without the large footprints needed today.

Conversely, we will want to degrade our adversaries' battlespace awareness. Requirements depend upon our ability to effectively manage battlespace information. Our current approach to command and control (and organizations) has been designed to keep the span of control within well-known human limits. As we have seen, the traditional response to the proliferation of entities requiring management is to add layers to the hierarchy, keeping the span of control manageable. This is an unacceptable response in the Information Age because it adversely affects the agility of the organization and slows the flow of information, both of which are vital to an Information Age enterprise. New approaches to command and new command arrangements are needed to effectively flatten hierarchies, free information flow (not orders) from the chain of command, and enable the enterprise to increase the speed of command to lock out adversarial options and achieve option dominance.

When sensors and actors are decoupled from one another and their supporting platforms, there will be a great increase in the number of battlespace entities that need to be managed. The pressures on Information Age organizations to reduce, not add, layers makes it important to develop new approaches to command and control that can handle very large numbers of battlespace entities, while at the same time increasing organizational agility. The answer can be found in an altered notion of control that is inspired by the study of chaos and complexity.[51] The next section explores these issues.

The Shift to Network-Centric Operations

Although the broad tapestry of network-centric concepts is still emerging, there is clear evidence that a shift to network-centric operations has begun. The U.S. Navy's Cooperative Engagement Capability has demonstrated the increased combat power associated with the robust networking of sensors, shooters, and C2 capabilities in an Air Defense context. In the Tactical Warning and Attack Assessment mission area, Air Force Space Command's Attack and Launch Early Reporting to Theater (ALERT) capability is demonstrating the operational benefit of the robust networking of sensors in increasing battlespace awareness. The Space Based Infrared System, currently under development, exploits this same theme. In other mission areas, such as the Joint Suppression of Enemy Air Defense (JSEAD), ongoing Joint and Service experimentation explores concepts for robustly networked forces to increase combat power.[52]

Joint and Service doctrine incorporating network-centric warfighting concepts is beginning to emerge. This doctrine is being developed in order to accelerate the pace of movement of forces, maintain an unrelenting operational tempo, and decisively engage the enemy at the time and place of our choosing.[53] The operational level of war revolves around commanders, their staffs, and their relationships with other elements of the warfighting ecosystem. The shift to network-centric operations has the potential to not only change existing command relationships, but to create new kinds of command relationships, as well as new types of commanders.[54] For example, the concept of a sensor network commander, with responsibilities for synchronizing battlespace with military operations across a Joint battlespace, has been explored in the wargaming environment.[55]

At the strategic level, senior leaders and leading military strategists are asserting the potential for the cumulative effect of closely spaced events (such as a rapid sequence of local tactical disasters, occurring over a period of hours) to dislocate and confuse an enemy to the point that his warfighting structures quickly disintegrate, and his feasible courses of action are rapidly reduced, resulting in an unequivocal military decision with minimum cost to both sides.[56] Realizing this potential will require a focused effort to work closely with allied and coalition partners as we move forward with Network Centric Warfare.[57] These developments are not lost on existing and potential adversaries, some of who are already demonstrating the capability to network their forces to increase combat power.[58]

In recent years we have witnessed a blurring of the distinctions among the levels of warfare. In particular, we have seen how what would have been considered relatively minor tactical events, or events with minor military significance (e.g., the loss of 18 American soldiers in Mogadishu, Somolia, in October 1993; the accidental bombing of the Chinese Embassy by Allied

Forces in Belgrade in May 1999 during *Operation Noble Anvil*; and the SCUD attacks against Israeli cities in the Gulf War) have had significant strategic implications. NCW, with the significantly improved capabilities that it brings to the table (in some mission areas, an order of magnitude increase in combat power), has the potential to significantly impact the outcome of military operations and enable commanders to change their operational and strategic calculus. For example, by increasing battlespace awareness, creating shared awareness, and helping to ensure that the most accurate information is made available to those who need it, situations like those that arose in Mogadishu, Belgrade, and the Gulf War can be avoided in the future, or have more favorable outcomes. Similarly, it is clear that an improved capability for performing the Joint Suppression of Enemy Air Defense Mission during *Operation Noble Anvil* would have had significant impact on the conduct of military operations.

However, this is not the only relationship between NCW and the coupling of tactical, operational, and strategic levels of war. Historically, these levels exist because of limitations in communications and span of control. As NCW lessens these constraints, we will be free to organize and operate differently. One can reasonably expect that some of the existing allocation of responsibilities among the levels of warfare will be modified as a result. This is something we need to keep our eyes on as Joint and Service experimentation proceeds.

Despite the immaturity of the Information Age and associated concepts like network-centric operations, efforts are being made to harness the opportunities they provide to generate value in the form of increased efficiencies and enhanced combat power. If history is a guide, the future will show that current efforts are tentative first steps and incremental improvements that barely scratch the surface. In the next chapter we step back and formally define Network Centric Warfare and examine its potential to create value for military organizations.

Network Centric Warfare

Network Centric Warfare (NCW) is based upon the experiences of organizations that have successfully adapted to the changing nature of their competitive spaces in the Information Age. One of the major lessons learned is that without changes in the way an organization does business, it is not possible to fully leverage the power of information. NCW recognizes the centrality of information and its potential as a source of power. This potential is realized as a direct result of the new relationships among individuals, organizations, and processes that are developed. These new relationships create new behaviors and modes of operation. It is the cumulative impact of new relationships among warfighting organizations that are the source of increased combat power.

NCW provides a new conceptual framework with which to examine military missions, operations, and organizations. It is intended to provide a fresh perspective to help ensure that new approaches and solutions will not be constrained by outmoded ideas.

This chapter begins by defining Network Centric Warfare and explaining its fundamentals. This is followed by a discussion of the power of the network-centric approach to operations and organizations, and the manner in which this power is generated. The chapter concludes with a look at battlespace entities through the lens of NCW.

Definition of Network Centric Warfare

NCW is about human and organizational behavior. NCW is based on adopting a new way of thinking— network-centric thinking—and applying it to military operations. NCW focuses on the combat power that can be generated from the effective linking or networking of the warfighting enterprise. It is characterized by the ability of geographically dispersed forces (consisting of entities) to create a high level of shared battlespace awareness that can be exploited via self-synchronization and other network-centric operations to achieve commanders' intent.[59] NCW supports speed of command—the conversion of superior information position to action. NCW is transparent to mission, force size, and geography. Furthermore, NCW has the potential to contribute to the coalescence of the tactical, operational, and strategic levels of war. In brief, NCW is not narrowly about technology, but broadly about an emerging military response to the Information Age.

Figure 9, The Military as a Network-Centric Enterprise, relates the basic elements necessary to generate combat power to the Network-Centric Enterprise model discussed earlier. As in the commercial sector, it all begins with infostructure. This in turn enables the creation of shared battlespace awareness and knowledge. This awareness and knowledge is leveraged by new adaptive command and control approaches and self-synchronizing forces. The "bottom line" here is increased tempo of

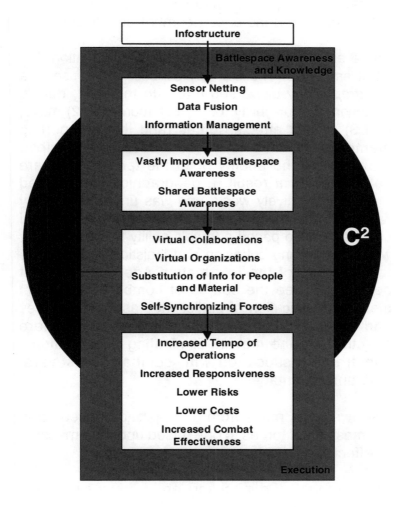

Figure 9. The Military as a Network-Centric Enterprise

operations, increased responsiveness, lower risks, lower costs, and increased combat effectiveness.

There are several key concepts in this definition that merit emphasis. The first key concept is the use of a *geographically dispersed* force. In the past, due to limitations in our ability to: 1) communicate, 2) move, and 3) project effects, forces (and their supporting elements) needed to be co-located, or in close proximity, to the enemy or to the target they were defending. As a result, a geographically dispersed force was relatively weak, and was unable to quickly respond to or mount a concentrated attack. Locational constraints also paced a force's ability to move rapidly while maintaining cohesion and logistics support. The technologies of the Information Age have made it possible to free the source of combat power from the physical location of battlespace assets or entities and may, in the future, allow forces to be more effective "on the move." Eliminating geo-locational constraints associated with combat has several inherent advantages.

It allows us to move from an approach based upon the massing of forces to one based upon the massing of effects.

As the ranges of our sensors and weapons increase and as our ability to move information rapidly improves, we are no longer geographically constrained. Hence, in order to generate a concentrated effect, it is no longer necessary to concentrate forces.

This allows us to reduce our battlespace footprint, which in turn reduces risk because we avoid presenting the enemy with attractive, high-value targets. It also expands the concept of maneuver by reducing the need for the transportation or movement of physical objects, a very time-consuming and expensive task. With NCW, we really can have the same thing in more than one place at the same time. This is because a sensor or shooter can now be in a position to engage many different targets without having to move.

The second key concept is the fact that our force is *knowledgeable*. Empowered by knowledge, derived from a shared awareness of the battlespace and a shared understanding of commanders' intent, our forces will be able to self-synchronize, operate with a small footprint, and be more effective when operating autonomously. A knowledgeable force depends upon a steady diet of timely, accurate information, and the processing power, tools, and expertise necessary to put battlespace information into context and turn it into battlespace knowledge.

The third key concept is that there is *effective linking* achieved among entities in the battlespace. This means that:

1) dispersed and distributed entities can generate synergy, and
2) that responsibility and work can be dynamically reallocated to adapt to the situation.

Effective linking requires the establishment of a robust, high-performance information infrastructure, or *infostructure*, that provides all elements of the warfighting enterprise with access to high-quality information services.

The effectiveness of linking mechanisms and processes affects the power coefficient or multiplier. The nature of the links that will provide the best performance under a wide range of battlespace environments and conditions is one of the key questions that needs to be addressed as we take NCW from concept to reality. A word of caution— closer linking is not necessarily better for all battlespace entities or mission circumstances. There is no intrinsic value to be had for tightly coupled links; rather, the goal is to build the configuration that creates the most effective force.

Settling on a term to describe the likely nature of warfare in the Information Age has been difficult, with each suggested term having its shortcomings. Network Centric Warfare, as we define it, is the most appropriate term that has been suggested so far because it directly, or indirectly, recognizes the essential characteristics of the revolution taking place in the commercial sector that will be manifested in warfare in the Information Age.[60] Network Centric Warfare recognizes the potential for the decoupling of sensors from actors, and each from platforms when it specifies a geographically dispersed force. It recognizes the centrality of information by specifying knowledgeable assets. NCW, by networking our forces, also focuses attention on the importance of the interactions among battlespace entities that are necessary to generate synergistic effects.

NCW, as a whole, has the characteristics necessary for coping with an increasingly important characteristic of warfare—its dynamic nature. NCW provides commanders with the flexibility to employ a broad range of command approaches from existing approaches to emerging concepts such as self-synchronization. This operational flexibility will be necessary to meet the challenges of the Information Age.

The term Network Centric Warfare also carries some baggage. By mistake, some have focused on communication networks, not on warfare or operations where the focus should rightly be. Networks are merely a means to an end; they convey "stuff" from one place to another and they are the purview of technologists. NCW does not focus on network-centric computing and communications, but rather focuses on information flows, the nature and characteristics of battlespace entities, and how they need to interact. NCW is all about deriving combat power from distributed interacting entities with significantly improved access to information. NCW reflects and incorporates the characteristics necessary for success in the Information Age—the characteristics of agility and the ability to capitalize on opportunities revealed by developing an understanding of the battlespace that is superior to that developed by an adversary.

Power of NCW

Specifically, as its name implies, NCW focuses on reaping the potential benefits of linking together—or networking—battlespace entities; that is, allowing them to work in concert to achieve synergistic effects (but not requiring them to always operate in a linked fashion). NCW is built around the concept of sharing information and assets. Networking enables this. A network consists of nodes (entities) and the links among them. Nodes do things (sense, decide, act) and information, both as inputs to decisions and in the form of decisions themselves, is passed over links from one battlespace entity, or node, to another.

Linking battlespace entities together will greatly increase warfighting effectiveness by allowing us to get more use out of our battlespace entities. The commercial experience has shown how information can substitute for material and how to move information instead of moving people. These substitutions generate considerable savings in time and resources and result in increased value in the form of combat power for a given level of investment.

We can understand the source of increased combat associated with network-centric operations by first examining the combat power of "platforms" or "nodes" operating in a stand-alone mode. In order to successfully engage a target, all of the following must be accomplished within a certain amount of time. First, the target must be detected. Second, it must be identified. Third, the decision to engage the target must be made. Fourth, the decision must be conveyed to a weapon. Fifth, the weapon must be aimed and fired. Associated with a particular engagement is a time budget and engagement range. The time budget varies greatly as a function of whether the target is mobile or employing countermeasures. The consumption of time depends upon the ranges of the sensors and weapons, kill radius of the weapons, time required to communicate and process information, and decision-making times required. The effective range depends upon both the range characteristics of the sensor(s) and weapons, as well as the effect of range on the consumption of time. Figure 10, Platform-Centric Shooter, portrays a platform-centric engagement where sensing and engagement capabilities reside on the same platform, and there is only limited capability for a weapons platform to engage a target based on awareness generated by other platforms. This figure describes the functional components of an engagement for a

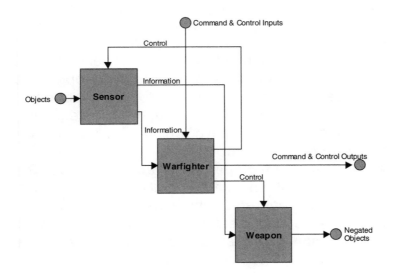

Figure 10. Platform-Centric Shooter

single warfighter on the ground, in a tank, flying an aircraft, or commanding a surface or subsurface combatant.

In combat operations, the performance capabilities of a sensor-weapon combination are governed to the first order by the geometric argument portrayed in Figure 11, Platform-Centric Engagement Envelope. In this figure, the sensing envelope is represented by a circle, and the maximum weapons employment envelope by a shaded circle. In platform-centric operations, value in the form of combat power can be created only when the platforms onboard sensor provides engagement quality awareness to the warfighter and the target is within the weapons maximum employment envelope. The effective engagement envelope is the area defined by the overlap of engagement quality awareness and the weapons maximum employment envelope. The effective engagement envelope, or E^3, is portrayed as the shaded area of the diagram. Consequently, the instantaneous combat power for a platform-centric engagement is proportional to the effective engagement envelope. As is apparent from the diagram, in platform-centric operations, combat power is often marginalized by the inability of the platform to generate engagement quality awareness at ranges greater than or equal to the maximum weapons employment envelope. This situation occurs frequently in platform-centric air engagements, as a result of the inability of an aircrew to positively identify as friend or foe the objects that they can detect and track at the full range of their sensors.

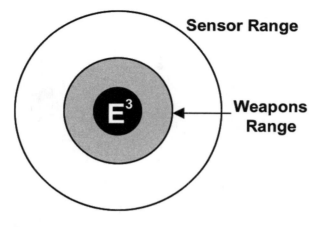

Figure 11. Platform-Centric Engagement Envelope

In the vast majority of combat operations, shooters are employed in conjunction with command and control capabilities. The operational situation that exists when platform-centric shooters are linked to a command and control node with sensing capabilities via a voice link is portrayed in Figure 12, C2 and Platform-Centric Shooters. The C2 node is capable of developing a finite level of awareness based on information provided by sensors, which may be colocated with the C2 node or external to the C2 node. In most cases, the level of awareness available to the C2 node is of sufficient quality to vector a shooter to an engagement zone, but not of sufficient quality to enable a shooter to engage directly. Furthermore, since the link between the C2 platform and the platform-centric shooter is a voice link, all information exchanges between the C2 node and shooter must take place via voice.

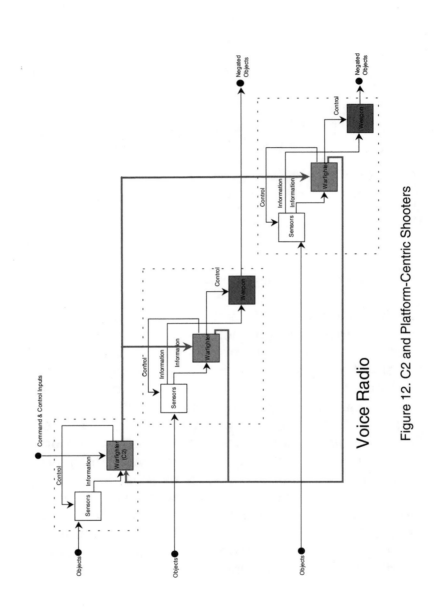

Figure 12. C2 and Platform-Centric Shooters

For example, in counter-air operations, a weapons controller onboard an E-2 Hawkeye or E-3 AWACS (Airborne Warning and Control System) does not necessarily have engagement quality awareness on all objects that it has in track. Typically, either the uncertainty associated with the position of the potential target is large or insufficient information is available to positively identify a target. Consequently, the crew of the "shooting" aircraft must employ sensors onboard the aircraft to develop engagement quality awareness (in some cases this may require performing a visual ID) and engage the target with onboard weapons. Furthermore, since all information exchanges are taking place via voice, it can be extremely difficult for the crews of the C2 node and platform-centric shooters to develop and maintain situational awareness when there are large numbers of blue and red forces operating in close proximity,

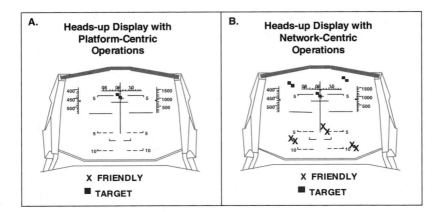

Figure 13. Platform-Centric Operations
vs. Network-Centric Operations

as depicted in Figure 13A, Heads-up Display with Platform-Centric Operations.

In contrast, network-centric operations are portrayed in Figure 14. In NCW, capabilities for sensing, commanding, controlling, and engaging are robustly networked via digital data links. The source of the increased power in a network-centric operation is derived in part from the increased content, quality, and timeliness of information flowing between the nodes in the network. This increased information flow is key to enabling shared battlespace awareness, and increasing the accuracy of the information as portrayed in Figure 13B, Heads-up Display with Network-Centric Operations.

Operational experience with tactical data links provides an existence proof for the power of network-centric operations. In an experiment which compared the operational performance of Air Force F-15Cs performing counter air operations with and without data links, the Air Force found that the kill ratio increased by over 100 percent with network-centric operations. This increased combat power resulted from the significantly enhanced battlespace awareness that was provided to the pilots operating with tactical data links. Components of awareness included weapons loading of the blue force, real-time position of the blue and red force, and status of blue engagements. The net result was a significantly improved capability for observing, orienting, deciding, and acting. Findings from recent All Service Combat Identification Evaluation Team (ASCIET) Exercises reinforce these findings.

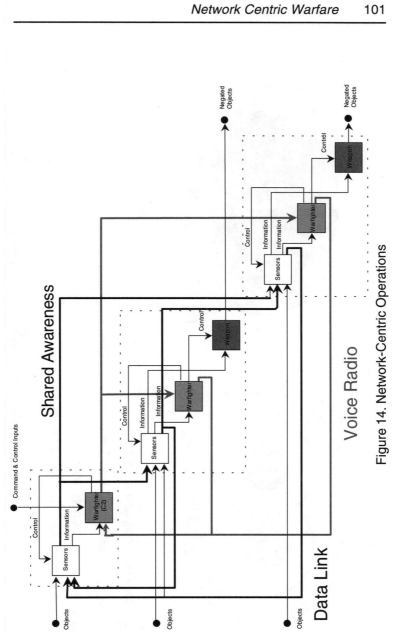

Figure 14. Network-Centric Operations

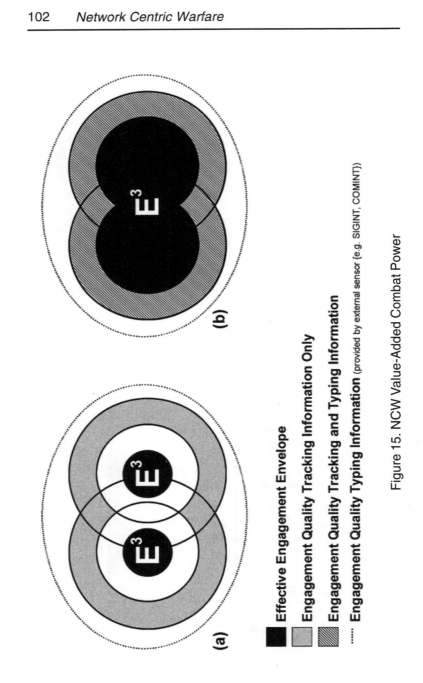

Figure 15. NCW Value-Added Combat Power

Figure 15 compares a case (a) that portrays two platform-centric shooters operating in close proximity, supported by an external sensing capability that can provide typing information. In this operational situation, real-time engagement information cannot be shared effectively and combat power is not maximized. In contrast, (b) portrays a geometric argument for the value-added combat power associated with a network-centric operation.

In this mode of operation, near real-time information sharing among nodes enables potential combat power to be increased. The robust networking of sensors provides the force with the capability to generate shared awareness with increased quality. This increase in awareness is proportional to the total area covered by the sensor zones. This increased awareness can be exploited by the robust networking of C2 and actor entities, which enables cooperative execution and self-synchronization of forces. The potential increase in total combat power associated with a network-centric operation is represented by the increased area of the effective engagement envelope. This simple example illustrates the application of Metcalfe's Law to military operations.

A word of caution is appropriate here. Metcalfe's Law is really about potential gains; there is no guarantee that simply hooking things up across the battlespace without appropriate organizational and doctrinal changes will increase warfighting effectiveness. In fact, there is every possibility that the unintended consequences of wiring up the battlespace and hoping for the best will, in fact, degrade performance particularly if doctrine, organization, training, and other key elements of the process are now changed to take advantage of the new configuration.[61] Therefore, the road to warfare based upon NCW needs to be richly populated with analyses and experiments in order to understand how we can reap the huge potential of NCW, while avoiding the pitfalls of unintended consequences.

The extent to which a network's productivity exceeds the sum of the productivity of its parts depends upon two things. The first is the gain that can be achieved by simply sharing resources (information) among the nodes. To illustrate this point, consider an example (over-simplified to make the point) in which organizations or individuals are distributed globally, each having a relatively small probability of possessing a given piece of information that is needed to make a plan successful. Let us say that this probability is 5 percent. If the planner only has access to organic information, he would only have a 5 percent chance of generating a successful plan. If the planner has access to the information that is available to a second organization, the chance he would get the information he needed to make the plan successful would be about 10 percent.

In general, for n sources the answer is $[1-.95^n]$. For n=5, the probability of having the information necessary to develop a successful plan is .226; for n=10 it is .401; and for n=25 the odds start to look much better at .723. Obviously, not all organizations have an equal probability of having the needed information. This actually works in our favor, provided we use our knowledge about which organizations and individuals are most likely to have the information needed. Given the development of reach-back capabilities, anchor desks, and smart information collection plans (or agents), we can, using the power of a network, turn a very low probability of having the information we need to a relatively high probability event.

This is what most people think about when they think about the power of a network. But there is also a fundamental new hypothesis that suggests that unlocking the full power of the network also involves our ability to affect the nature of the decisions that are inherently made by the network, or made collectively, rather than being made by an individual entity. This may not be immediately clear since these collective decisions are often implicit, and therefore not very visible. They have not been studied adequately, the focus to date being on explicit decision making. What this hypothesis implies is that we need to focus more attention on the behavior of the networked entities rather than just studying and considering the behavior of individual entities. Findings from *Fleet Battle Experiment Delta*, which will be discussed in more detail later, lend support to this hypothesis.

It is axiomatic, given almost any problem (e.g., assigning actors to targets), that one can always do as well, if not better, if a constraint is relaxed (again the ability is there, not the guarantee). However, constraints are often used as a means to achieve ends that are often as important as the objective of the task at hand. For example, given the problem of assigning actors to targets, constraints on the options are often used as a means to reduce fratricide, even though they will reduce the number of targets killed and increase leakage. The goal of NCW in this case is to achieve a reduction in fratricide while minimizing the constraints placed upon the weapons. One way to achieve this is to make actors more knowledgeable and their weapons smarter by providing them with more information.

To illustrate the power derived from sharing information, take the problem of assigning targets to actors. This problem can be formulated either as a centralized (unconstrained) or a decentralized (constrained) problem. That is, either there is:

1) one decision maker with no constraints on the information or processing power available to this decision maker, or on the decision maker's ability to communicate; or

2) there are several decision makers, each with limited vision and limited processing power (the sum of which may actually exceed that of the single decision maker).

Let us consider the case where a single decision maker could have the collective knowledge of targets; a unified picture of the battlespace and the time needed to process all of the information and transmit targeting orders to each actor. Under these conditions, an "optimal" decision could be reached. The function of the network in this case is to bring together partial pictures, assemble them into a unified whole, and then convey the product of the decision-making process to each actor. In other words, the sensor nodes share their information with the decision node, which in turn shares the decision with the actor nodes. Reality conspires against us and we rarely, if ever, are able to centralize collection and decision making to this degree. Thus, we rarely make "optimal" decisions. To some the goal of centralized optimal decisions remains at the heart of their vision of the future. For us it does not.

We see the power of NCW being derived from empowering all the decision makers in the battlespace rather than just a few. The realities of complexity and battle tempo will drive us to this use of the network. The objective is to get all our players and assets into the game at the same time. The ability to hit many high-value targets simultaneously gives us the wherewithal to employ a strategy of shock and awe that can bring a situation to a conclusion far more rapidly than an attrition-based approach.

Thus, contrary to some expressed concerns, NCW does not inevitably take us down the road to centralized control. In fact, from the explorations conducted so far it seems to be taking us down the road to increased (improved) awareness for all players with more collaboration and decentralization in the form of self-synchronizing forces.[62] As we apply the concepts of NCW to the "management" of battlespace information, we can expect that, in absolute terms, everyone will be more knowledgeable about the battlespace of the future than even some, if not all of, the best-informed entities are today. In the future we can expect tactical level commanders will have a better understanding of both the big picture and the local situation than operational level commanders currently have today.

The potential for information overload is real and great care must be taken to make sure that what is provided is actually information and not noise.[63] In addition, access to tools and expertise will be required to achieve battlespace knowledge. What is of value and what is likely to distract depend to a great extent upon what the entity is supposed to do. Part of the challenge faced will be to develop a better understanding of situational needs and to provide the necessary education and training to deal with the explosion of information.

Virtual Collaboration

In this chapter, we have examined the nature of the benefits that can be obtained by sharing information and assets. Earlier the point was made that the robust networking of the warfighting ecosystem enables new kinds of relationships to develop. One of the most powerful relationships that emerges is virtual collaboration. Virtual collaboration goes far beyond simple sharing of information. It enables elements of the warfighting ecosystem to interact and collaborate in the virtual domain, moving information instead of moving people and achieving a critical knowledge mass. Key component technologies such as video teleconferencing (VTC), virtual whiteboards, and collaborative planning applications enable virtual collaboration.

Virtual collaboration in the information domain has numerous operational benefits. For example, virtual collaboration enables the times associated with existing planning and execution process to be reduced. These savings provide additional time to rehearse, move to contact, or sleep. The net result is increased effectiveness.

In Expeditionary Aerospace Operations, moving information instead of people changes the dynamics of the force deployment process by enabling split base operations. The concept has proven to be promising during *Expeditionary Force Experiment '98*. Split base operations has the potential to both decrease the time required to initiate air operations and free up transport aircraft to move combat capability into theater. The ability to move information instead of people also has significant benefits in other areas. The seven examples that follow highlight some of the benefits of the shift to network-centric operations.

Example 1: *New Relationships Between Commanders—Battle Command via VTC*

Old Way: Corps and division commanders travel across the battlefield to be in the same place at the same time to plan ground operations.

Network Centric Warfare: Commanders interact via VTC, which results in a significant reduction in planning time and elimination of time to travel.

Value: Decreased planning time provides commanders with the operational flexibility to enable their forces to rehearse, move to contact, re-supply, repair, or rest. Net result is increased combat power.

Concept Status: Demonstrated by U.S. Army in operational exercises.

Example 2: *Split Base Operations*

Old Way: Air Force deploys 1,500 to 2,000 warriors into theater to set up and operate a Joint Air Operations Center. Moving the personnel and equipment requires 25 C-17 missions and takes over 10 to 15 days.

Network Centric Warfare: Air Force moves an order of magnitude less people into theater to operate a Forward Joint Air Operations Center (JAOC), which is supported by a robustly networked force in the form of a Distributed Air Operations Center based in CONUS. With a significantly reduced logistics footprint, the forward JAOC can be deployed into theater with less than five C-17 missions and be operational in 24 to 48 hours from receipt of deployment order.[64] This concept is portrayed in Figure 16.

Value: Air Operations Center is operational in 24 to 48 hours, enabling operational commander to more effectively employ expeditionary Air Forces moving into theater. Furthermore, the C-17 missions which are freed up can carry enough material to deploy two Tactical Fighter Wings into theater.

Concept Status: Explored by the U.S. Air Force in *Expeditionary Force Experiment '98.*

Example 3: *Virtual Support Services*

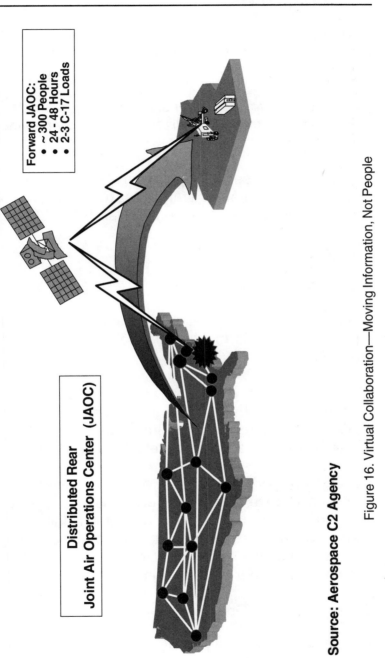

Figure 16. Virtual Collaboration—Moving Information, Not People

Source: Aerospace C2 Agency

Old Way: Supporting staff such as dispersing clerks, radiologists, and weather officers deploy with operational units.

Network-Centric Operations: Specialists provide virtual services from centralized locations by moving information.

Value: Improved services, provided at reduced costs, enabled by massing of intellectual capital in centralized locations in the continental United States.

Concept Status: Operational.

Example 4: *Quality of Life*

Old Way: Deployed forces communicate with families and loved ones via mail or telephone, at infrequent intervals.

Network-Centric Operations: Deployed forces communicate with families and loved ones with increased frequency and timeliness via e-mail (potentially on a daily basis), telephone, or VTC.[65]

Value: Deployed warfighters are able to solve family problems in close to real time (e.g., finance), interact with their children, and experience their children's lives while they are growing up. Worry goes down, morale goes up, and operational effectiveness remains at a higher level over long deployments.[66]

Concept Status: Operational.

Example 5: *Distance Learning*

Old Way: Units release warfighters to attend training or education events away from their units.

Network-Centric Operations: Education is provided to warfighters deployed with their units via VTC or compact disk (CD).[67]

Value: Manning levels are maintained and opportunities for education and training are available to all deployed forces. Operational proficiency and morale increase.

Concept Status: Operational.

Example 6: *Collaborative Mission Planning*

Old Way: A complex multi-aircraft strike takes hours to days to plan employing traditional techniques. The challenges of synchronizing and de-conflicting multiple strike packages require multiple planning iterations.

Network Centric Warfare: Collaborative planning tools enable strike planners, potentially based on multiple ships or in units ashore, to plan and de-conflict multi-aircraft strike packages.[68]

Value: Improved capabilities for synchronization and de-confliction significantly decrease planning time and provide aircrews with the operational flexibility to rehearse or accelerate operational tempo. Net result is increased combat power.

Concept Status: Operational.

Example 7: *Joint Intelligence Virtual Architecture (JIVA)—Virtual Collaboration for Intelligence*

Old Way: Intelligence analysts operating in geographically distributed locations have a limited capability to interact and collaborate on intelligence products. Stove-piped intelligence dissemination systems limit access to intelligence products and provide a limited capability to search or browse databases and perform comparative analysis.

Network-Centric Operations: Collaborative tools enable intelligence analysts based worldwide to collaborate in the development of intelligence products. Sophisticated data mining and data warehousing applications provide intelligence analysts with significantly improved access to large volumes of source data for analysis and integration.

Value: Significantly improved intelligence products and worldwide access to these products.

Concept Status: Ongoing development and deployment in the Intelligence community.

Battlespace Entities

The task at hand is to design a set of battlespace entities and a set of interconnections (an enterprise of networked or linked entities) that can take full advantage of the increased amount of information available, turn this information into knowledge, and generate increased combat power. In other words, leverage shared battlespace awareness to allocate, assign, and employ assets and then modify these allocations, assignments, and employments as awareness of the situation changes. In some operational situations, a desired objective is to achieve battlefield results that approach a *global optima* without using a centralized approach, thus avoiding the significant shortcomings associated with centralized approaches. In other operational situations, a premium must be placed on flexibility and adaptability vice solely focusing on optimization. Consequently, the concept of *dynamic fitness* must play a key role in both the design and employment of forces.

Transforming NCW from a concept into a reality requires that we define the battlespace entities (their roles, responsibilities, tasks, and decisions), their connectivity (links among them), and the nature of the information and products that are exchanged (the degree of coupling).

It is the extent and nature of the interactions among battlespace entities that generate the power of

NCW.[69] We have chosen to focus this discussion on battlespace entities somewhat abstractly to illuminate the underlying fundamentals of NCW. Battlespace entities have three primary functional modes: sensing, deciding, and acting. The degree to which one functional mode dominates at a particular point in time determines the role of an entity in a military operation. Entities that have a primary function of sensing are called sensors. Sensors include all entities that contribute to battlespace awareness, from satellites to "eyes on the ground." Actors are those entities that have the promary function of creating "value" in the form of "combat power" in the battlespace. Actors employ both traditional (lethal) and nontraditional (nonlethal) means. Decision makers perform a variety of functions (e.g., making resource allocation decisions) and are found at all levels of the organization. Battlespace entities will need to be connected in some fashion, but how they need to be connected is not predetermined. Moreover, we do not want to imply a universal connectivity where every node is directly connected to every other node, or that all nodes are provided with the same level of information services. That being said, NCW is based upon sharing information and assets to achieve synergistic, collaborative effects, and it is unlikely that the proper degree of coupling can be realized without having a high-performance, communications, and computational capability providing access to appropriate information sources, and allowing seamless interactions among battlespace entities in a "plug and play" fashion. This is called the "infostructure." Determining the nature of this enabling infostructure and the best way to acquire it present significant challenges.

There has been a tendency, in the effort to explain NCW, for its proponents to speak in conceptual terms, and others to hear in literal terms. NCW can only be effectively reduced to simple vu-graphs if everyone understands that the links portrayed are only notional, and that in reality it is the specifics that count—which links exist, what information is passed, and what is done with the information.

It is not hard to understand a battlespace with three kinds of entities. Everyone seems to understand that these can be located throughout the battlespace (either in fixed locations or increasingly as mobile) and that a wide variety of sensors would exist. Further, there seems to be no difficulty when it comes to the notion that some entities may, in fact, have complex functionality—e.g., perform the roles of sensing and acting at the same time. The difficulty seems to be in understanding the nature of the links among entities, and in appreciating the combat power associated with the network-centric operations that the links enable.

The nature of the connectivity and the division of responsibilities remain the central issues that need to be explored as experimentation with NCW begins. It is here that some confusion exists. This confusion is a result of the tendency to move from the specific to the collective as the discussion shifts from entities to links.

From this collective, or global, vantage point a collection of sensors (or as it is often depicted, a "network of sensors") can be viewed as providing the information from which battlespace awareness is generated. This sort of picture implies that somehow all of the sensors are actually linked together. While this makes sense conceptually, it may not make sense in practice. NCW focuses attention both on the appropriate linking of sensor entities, and on the contributions they make to generating shared battlespace awareness. Developing shared battlespace awareness requires that sensor entities (or rather the information they generate) be linked in some fashion. This does not mean that all sensor entities need to be *directly* linked to one another; neither does this mean that they all need to be linked into a single sensor network. In most cases, sensor networks require only that a subset of battlespace sensors be task organized and provided with high performance information services. Shared battlespace awareness requires that the information collected by sensors be put in a form that makes it possible for other battlespace entities (but not necessarily all others) to fuse appropriate information, place it in context, and understand its implications. This will permit the sharing of information that is so important to begin reaping the potential power of NCW.

From a global vantage point, battlespace awareness seems as if it exists as a single thing. Battlespace awareness really exists in a distributed form. We really only see a slice of it at one time—either a particular detail or a gross overview without details. In fact, research results indicate that the ability to move up and down levels of abstraction without introducing distortions distinguishes effective from ineffective utilization of knowledge. This tendency in discussing NCW to move from the global or collective vantage point (where we consider conceptual relationships) to the specifics (where we think about actual links among entities) has created confusion about what NCW really means and the ways to achieve it.

In the same way that sensor entities will be linked to many more entities than they currently are, so will actor entities be more richly linked as well. Again, this does not imply all actors will be linked to an actor network, or exclusively or primarily to other actors. Rather that actors (e.g., shooters) will have a far richer collection of links to other battlespace entities than they do with platform-centric operations. In the future they will be linked to each other, directly to sensor entities, or indirectly to sensor entities by virtue of having direct access to their products (individually and/or collectively).

The purpose of linking actor entities in this fashion is to make them better informed and to increase their overall effectiveness. Making them better informed means they need to know more not only about the classification and position of enemy assets, but also about a host of other things. For example, they need to know the overall situation, the commander's intent, the current and planned positions, and the intended actions of other battlespace entities, including neutrals. With this increased knowledge comes better understanding, which carries with it the ability to do a better job of developing insights, and generating combat power.

This brings us to the relationships that sensor and actor entities will have with decision (or command) entities. Obviously, decision entities must be linked to both sensor and actor entities, as well as to other decision entities. The link between a decision entity and a sensor entity (or entities) can be either direct or indirect. The link may transfer raw data or products. It may be one-way, two-way, or interactive. These are only some of the possibilities. Decision entities may be linked to other decision entities and actors in a similar variety of ways.

NCW has often been articulated somewhat abstractly where sensors and actors are richly interconnected. This is a conceptual representation and should not be taken literally. The point to be made is that information collected by sensors can be brought to bear in a far more flexible way than is currently possible, with the selection of the actor not being as restricted as it currently is in platform-centric configurations.

A major difference between NCW and traditional approaches to warfare is that in NCW, actors (shooters) do not inherently own sensors, and decision makers do not inherently own actors. In platform-centric operations, platforms own weapons and weapons have their own organic sensors. For example, in the Air Defense Mission Area, the commander of a Hawk Missile Battery has dedicated sensors and absolute control over the employment of his missiles. His organic sensing capabilities cannot be exploited by others and his weapons cannot be assigned by others. In contrast, with NCW, all three types of entities work collaboratively in response to the dynamics of the battlespace to achieve commanders' intent. This enables decision and actor entities to play a wide variety of roles. The net result will be a dynamically re-configurable force that can take on the characteristics best suited for fast-paced battlespace domains where opportunities are fleeting and delay can be fatal. Continuing the Air Defense example with network-centric operations, the operational constraints that are currently associated with platform-centric operations may be eliminated in situations when it would make sense for a Hawk Missile Battery's sensors or missiles to be tasked by another battlespace entity, such as a commander with responsibilities for the Joint Theater Air and Missile Defense Mission.

This does not imply that it is a "free for all" on the battlefield; rather, the point is that all assets can be employed more flexibly, resulting in a more agile force. Exactly how this aspect of NCW will work remains to be developed as part of the implementation of JV2010, particularly the series of Joint experiments that will be an integral part of this process. NCW is offered to provide a rich source of hypotheses to be tested and refined, and a conceptual framework to focus the experiments and analyses ahead.

We have seen how NCW frees us from a host of constraints that currently restrict how we use the information our sensors generate, and how we employ our actors. We also have seen how breaking down these constraints offers the opportunity to reap the power of the network that is inherent in Metcalfe's Law. In the next chapter, the roles of battlespace entities are discussed in detail, and the coupling of these entities, combined with increases in weapons reach, improved maneuverability of armored forces, and enhanced precision weapons, will enable a vastly increased speed of command which can generate more force effects in a given period of time.

Although we still have a tendency to use the vocabulary of combat at the tactical level, NCW is applicable to all levels of warfare and contributes to the coalescence of strategy, operations, and tactics. Its ability to contribute to military operations by increasing shared awareness extends to a wide variety of missions, force sizes, and force compositions.

Roles of Battlespace Entities

E ach of the entities in the battlespace can add value to the mission by contributing to:

1) Battlespace awareness and knowledge
2) Command and control and decision making
3) Execution

Thus, generally speaking, the collection of sensor entities contributes information which forms the basis for battlespace awareness and knowledge; the set of decision entities collectively exercises command and control by accomplishing planning and battle management; and the collection of actors executes the plan. The Information Age, however, is already bringing about changes that will ultimately merge battle management, planning, and execution into an integrated, dynamic adaptive progress. This will require effective interactions between not only decision entities and actors, but also sensors.

Figure 17, Roles of Battlespace Entities, depicts the respective roles and nature of the interactions among sensor, actor, and decision entities as we close out the 20th century and project the 21st century. A number of common operational pictures (COPs)[70] are depicted, each one of which can have more than one view. A view is usually a subset of information in the COP aggregated and displayed in a particular way to support a decision or task. COPs serve to ensure there is functional consistency among the different views. Currently, COPs are mainly a work in progress. Significant inconsistencies still need to be addressed. How best to do this, and the problems associated with achieving a common perception of a situation, remain topics for research and experimentation.

In Figure 17, decision makers and actors are organized into a hierarchy (the triangle), and each entity is connected to other entities. Sensors provide the data they collect either to data storage centers that support one or more COPs, as well as directly to selected actors. Decision entities can task a limited number of sensors, view COPs, and direct (command and control) actors. The limits are a function of our legacy, stove-piped environment. Actors get the information they need in a number of ways, either directly from selected sensors, locally stored static databases, or by viewing selected COPs, which are constantly being updated. Actors can also contribute information to data centers and communicate with other actors, passing information or commands back and forth.

Figure 17 also depicts how we expect the relationships among battlespace entities to evolve over the next few decades (21st century) as we strive to increase our knowledge of the battlespace. Depicted are the:

1) increased linkages among battlespace entities existing in the 21st century;
2) integration of various COPs, resulting in fewer COPs, each with the ability to

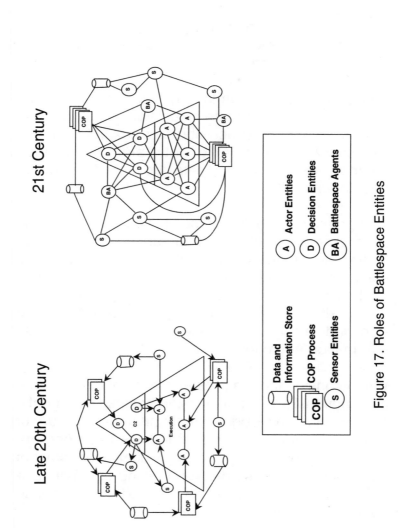

Figure 17. Roles of Battlespace Entities

provide an increased number of tailored views; and

3) introduction of battlespace agents which perform selected tasks as delegated by decision and actor entities.

These battlespace agents may take the form of any one of several automated decision or information processes, including decision aids, expert systems, trained neural nets, or genetic algorithms, each autonomously performing selected tasks for decision or actor entities.

To a great extent, only our imagination and willingness to employ them will limit the potential contribution of battlespace agents to the warfighting enterprise. The extent to which decisions will be delegated to agents will be hotly debated. However, we will, driven by the complexity and operating tempo of the Information Age, find it necessary to make judicious use of these Information Age capabilities in the 21st century.

When considering the pros and cons of delegating a particular task, or set of tasks, to battlespace agents, it is important to recognize that under the pressure of time or uncertainty, some of today's decisions are made either by default or by individuals who may not have all the expertise or even training or experience necessary to be proficient. Among the tasks that these agents are likely to perform are:

1) requesting additional information as required by the situation;
2) tasking sensors;

3) notifying decision entities of things that require immediate attention;
4) translating a commander's intent into messages or instructions implementing the intent;
5) identifying and resolving inconsistencies within a COP; and
6) developing and red teaming plans.

A discussion of the nature of the changes that can be expected in battlespace entities, and the links among them, is the subject of the next chapter. In turn, this chapter deals with the major tasks that need to be accomplished:

1) achieving battlespace awareness and knowledge;
2) providing command and control; and
3) execution and decision making.

The key to understanding the roles of and the relationships among battlespace entities is to focus on processes that turn raw data into information, and information into knowledge. Since each of these information-related terms is used rather loosely in everyday speech, and the two are often used interchangeably, we will briefly define this hierarchy of terms.

Data are individual facts, measurements, or observations which may or may not be sufficient to make a particular decision. Information is obtained when elements of data are assembled, reconciled, fused, and placed in an operational context. Knowledge is derived from being able to use information to construct and use an explanatory model based upon an understanding of the situation or phenomenon. Such a model allows us to forecast future states, predict outcomes, and also contributes to our ability to control the situation—or to be proactive rather than reactive. This is, of course, a primary goal of command and control.

Battlespace awareness results from the fusion of key elements of information which describe or characterize the battlespace. The elements are primarily explicit information (e.g., position of forces, geography, and weather). This type of information needs little interpretation and usually can be communicated quickly and easily. The vast majority of information in the common operational picture is explicit information. The difficulty comes in placing the information in a larger context and understanding its implications.

Sensor entities are key contributors to battlespace awareness. As is described in detail in the sections that follow, shared battlespace awareness is fundamentally a network-centric capability.

In contrast, battlespace knowledge consists of tacit information. Tacit information requires interpretations. While supporting "facts" can be easily transferred, the underlying organizing logic can seldom be transferred quickly and easily.[71] Examples of tacit information include capabilities and tactics of an adversary, local customs, and intent. Consequently, battlespace knowledge should be viewed as a people-centric capability in the sense that knowledge workers play a key role in developing, processing, and communicating tacit information.

Actor and decision entities can exploit battlespace awareness and knowledge by bringing various types of "models" to bear. They use doctrinal models, decision aids, expert systems, or the modeling services of an anchor desk that provides a reach-back capability to nondeployed entities. Hence, battlespace knowledge results in value added processes that use:

1) the experience of commanders and staffs; and
2) decision aids, simulation models, knowledge (expertise) located at a distance, and forms of AI and expert systems.

Actors can act upon any of these levels of information. However, their effectiveness in the specific and in the collective will differ as a function of the level of information that is acted upon and the timeliness of the actions. The tradeoff is between the quality of information available and the time to act. NCW should result in making more quality information available in a more timely manner.

Recent military operations in Kosovo during *Operation Noble Anvil* highlighted the power of new types of relationships among sensors, deciders, and actors that are possible with a network-centric force. Figure 18 portrays the information flow and operational tasks associated with the operation of the Predator UAV. The sensor was operated by actor entities located at one geographical location. The information collected by the sensor was analyzed by decision entities at multiple geographically dispersed locations. The information was then transmitted in near real time to decision entities located on command and control platforms and then to actor entities in the form of shooters, which engaged the targets sensed by the UAV.

In another operational situation, the roles of entities were reversed in real time to execute the mission. In this scenario, a pilot operating as the Forward Air Controller (FAC) (as a decision entity) had designated a target for engagement by a pilot operating strike aircraft (the actor). However, the strike aircraft had already expended the optimum weapon to engage the target, and its remaining weapons could not provide the required lethality. However, the aircraft operating as the FAC was loaded with munitions more appropriate for engaging the target. Consequently, the two aircraft switched roles. The strike aircraft took on the role of the FAC in designating the target, and the aircraft operating as the FAC engaged the target. When the engagement was complete, the aircraft operating initially in the role of the FAC reverted to operating in this role.

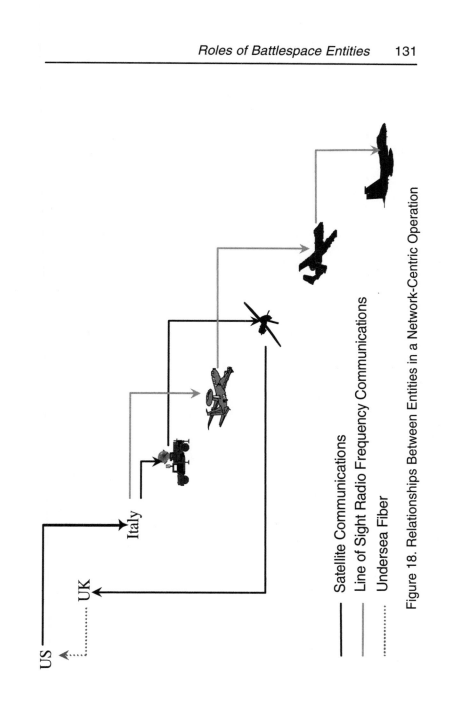

Figure 18. Relationships Between Entities in a Network-Centric Operation

Battlespace Awareness and Knowledge

A chieving high levels of battlespace awareness and knowledge lies at the foundation of Joint Vision 2010. NCW enhances the ability to develop and maintain battlespace awareness and knowledge by capitalizing on capabilities for collecting, processing, and transporting available information.

Battlespace knowledge is derived from shared battlespace awareness and involves the fusion of information into a set of COPs and the dissemination and display of COPs as shown in Figure 19. Providing battlespace awareness to warfighters across the Joint force with requisite accuracy and timeliness requires that data and information from multiple sources be collected, processed (analyzed when necessary), transported, fused, placed in appropriate contexts, and presented in ways that facilitate rapid and accurate inferences. It also requires that actors and decision entities be provided by training with internal models and/or decision aids or models. With this insight, we can observe that it requires both battlespace awareness and these cognitive models to generate battlespace knowledge which is in and of itself, an emergent network-centric property.

Examples of information concerning friendly, enemy, and neutral forces that can be integrated in a COP include:

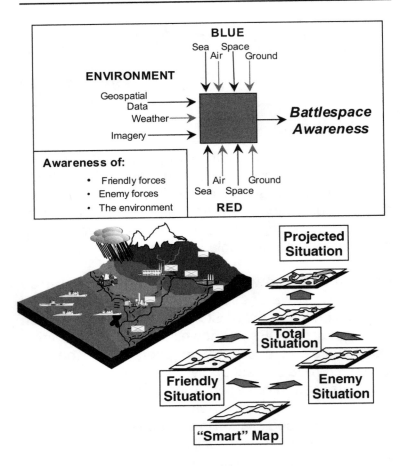

Figure 19. Elements of Battlespace Awareness

1) location (current positions, rate of
   movement, and predicted future
   positions);
2) status (readiness postures including
   combat capability, whether or not in
   contact, logistics sustainability, and so
   forth);

3) available courses of action and predicted actions for enemy forces (force information also includes the capabilities of offensive and defensive enemy weapons systems and damage assessment as a result of friendly actions);

4) the environment (including current and predicted weather conditions, the predicted effect of weather on planned operations and enemy options, and terrain features such as trafficability, canopy, sight lines, and sea conditions).

Shared battlespace awareness emerges when all relevant elements of the warfighting ecosystem are provided with access to the COP. This means that battlespace awareness must be viewed as a collective property (a type of collective consciousness). It does not exist at just one place (node) in the battlespace, but rather at all relevant nodes in the battlespace—across echelons and functional components. The degree of detail that is portrayed in an operational picture can and most likely will vary by echelon. For example, Figure 20 portrays a snapshot of the level of information provided by a COP available to the Brigade Commander during the Task Force XXI AWE. The degree to which the information content of an operational picture can vary across echelons to enable relevant information to be portrayed clearly and unambiguously to decision makers and actors is portrayed in Figure 21, Variation in Information Content for Operational Pictures.

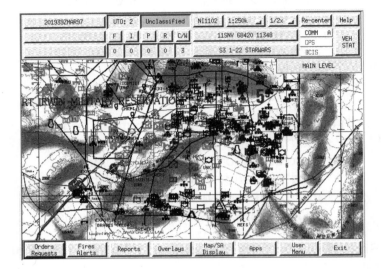

Figure 20. Common Operational Picture at the Brigade Level

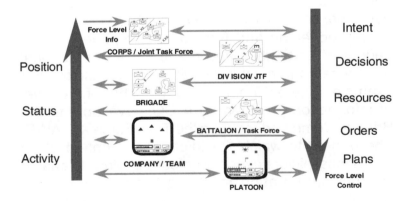

Figure 21. Variation in Information
Content for Operational Pictures

The information for generating battlespace awareness will be provided by numerous sources. For example, information on red forces can be collected by intelligence, surveillance, and reconnaissance platforms operating as part of a sensor network, sensors employed on weapons platforms, or human assets on the ground (e.g., manned reconnaissance teams). A shared awareness of blue positions across the battlespace can be generated by enabling all elements of the blue force to transmit their current position information and receive relevant position information from other entities. Each element of the blue force can establish its position in the battlespace with a high degree of accuracy through use of precision navigation systems like the global positioning system (GPS). Blue status information, such as fuel remining and weapons loading, can be generated using embedded sensors that track consumption of fuel and ordnance. Real-time operations data can also be collected (e.g., information on engine and transmission loading and use), which in turn can be employed to dynamically maintain current levels of operational readiness by more accurately predicting maintenance requirements. Environmental information can be collected with traditional sensor types (e.g., weather, imaging, ocean sensors, etc.), potentially augmented with information from sensors on weapons systems.

Generating shared awareness of blue requires that we have a mechanism in place to dynamically capture position, status, and intent information from all elements of the blue force and have the capability to provide relevant information on blue to those who need it. For this to happen, all relevant elements of the blue force need to be contributors to the process—they need to be connected to the network. In order to achieve battlefield awareness and then to achieve battlefield knowledge, we need to move beyond information that tells us where things are and provide information about their identities. It is also necessary to know something about current operational status and capabilities, as well as doctrine and intent.

Similarly, if information on red forces, or the environment, generated by a subset of the force (e.g., intelligence systems, sensors on board weapons platforms), is to be combined with blue force information to generate battlespace awareness, it needs to be distributed to all relevant elements of the warfighting force.

The ability to develop accurate and timely source information for battlespace awareness depends upon the characteristics of the information processes available and the performance of the network. For example, the accuracy of distributed position information on moving targets (friendly, neutral, red) is a function of not only collection and analysis processes, but also the relative velocity of objects and the velocity of information within the blue network.

For example, if a blue weapons platform, such as an AH-64D Longbow Apache, detects a column of tanks, its onboard sensor is capable of generating engagement quality information on most if not all of the tanks in the enemy formation. This information has significant potential value to the warfighting force. The value of this information is a function of who it can be shared with (e.g., decision and/or actor entities) and the timeliness of the information sharing. For example, if the Longbow Apache can transport engagement quality awareness to an artillery battery in real time, then the potential exists for the blue force to mass the effects of direct and indirect fires. If the information cannot be transmitted in real time, than an opportunity for massing effects is lost. However, if information on target positions collected by the Longbow Apache can be transmitted, but not in real time, the information may be accurate enough to enable close air support assets to subsequently acquire and engage the column of tanks.

Similarly, if a commander desires to increase the velocity of maneuver of his or her force and simultaneously maintain battlespace awareness, then the velocity of information must increase with the velocity of maneuver. For example, we can observe that as the average velocity of blue force increases, the instantaneous accuracy of shared position information will decrease if the average velocity of information does not increase as well. This occurs because instantaneous accuracy is a function of data latency. Simplified, using a constant position update rate, the instantaneous position error of a weapons platform, moving at 500 miles per hour (such as a fighter aircraft), is potentially 10 times larger than for a platform moving at 50 miles per hour (such as a tank).

In summary, the accuracy of the information in a COP is a function of the accuracy of source information, velocity of information between nodes in the network, and velocity of the objects of interest in the common operational picture.

Our ability to provide relevant battlespace entities with access to information can be exploited to increase the accuracy of our information about enemy assets. The specifics of how an increased velocity of information can be used to increase battlespace awareness is discussed below.

Sensor Networks

The operational performance of a sensor network (a collection of networked sensor entities) in generating battlespace awareness depends upon a number of factors including:

1) the performance of component sensors;
2) sensor geometry: the locations of the sensors with respect to each other and the objects of interest;
3) the velocity of information;
4) fusion capabilities; and
5) tasking capabilities.

In the fundamental shift to network-centric operations, sensor networks emerge as a key enabler of increased combat power. The operational value or benefit of sensor networks is derived from their enhanced ability to generate more complete, accurate, and timely information than can be generated by sensors operating in stand-alone mode. The performance advantage that emerges from the enabling of sensor networks is a function of the type of sensors being employed (e.g., active, passive) and the class of objects of interest (e.g., missiles, aircraft, tanks, submarines, etc.). Sensor networks can generate significantly increased battlespace awareness of objects in the battlespace.

Sensor networks provide significant performance advantages over stand-alone sensors in key mission spaces by overcoming the fundamental performance limitations (e.g., coverage, accuracy, and target identification properties) of individual stand-alone sensors. The value-adding processes of data fusion and sensor tasking can partially overcome these limitations. This does not imply that the level of awareness generated against all targets will be 100 percent in all mission areas, but rather that almost all mission areas can benefit to some degree from the shift to network-centric operations. A few examples follow.

Application of Sensor Networks to the Surveillance and Tracking of Objects in Air and Space

Active Sensors. Against objects moving in air and space, active radar sensors can provide very accurate ranging measurements and less accurate azimuth and bearing measurements. When errors in range and bearing are factored into estimation and prediction algorithms, the net result is an error ellipsoid which describes the uncertainty associated with a track in three dimensions. In addition, when radars are employed in the operational environment, scattering and environmental effects can combine to degrade the detection and tracking capabilities of stand-alone radar sensors, particularly against stressing targets (e.g., high speed, low observables).

Under operational conditions, the tracking performance of stand-alone sensors can degrade. This drop off in sensor performance can be manifested in track discontinuity, unacceptably slow track convergence, or in the worst case, inability to initiate a track. These performance limitations can be overcome by using information from two or more sensors, enabling data fusion and sensor tasking. Sensor fusion enables measurements from two or more sensors to develop a composite track. (This fusion process is portrayed in Figure 22.) The error ellipsoids that characterize the composite track converge much more rapidly to a level of accuracy that permits engagements (engagement quality awareness) when information from multiple sensors is available and utilized. Figure 23 portrays the ability of fusion to decrease the time required to generate engagement quality awareness.

Sensor tasking can further enhance performance. Sensor tasking enables sensor resources to be dynamically focused on high priority sectors of the battlespace. This enables a scarce sensor resource to serve many customers, and helps ensure that the right mix of sensors is available at the right time. For example, a stand-alone phased array radar exploits sensor tasking by tasking beams to operate in either broad area search mode or track mode. The operational benefit of sensor tasking is enhanced when sensors from multiple platforms simultaneously focus their energy on the same object. A functional model of the dynamic sensor tasking process is portrayed in Figure 24. The resulting increase in tracking performance, resulting from dynamic sensor

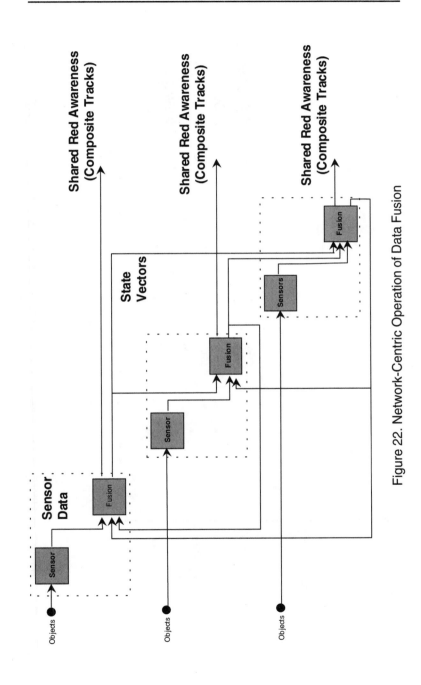

Figure 22. Network-Centric Operation of Data Fusion

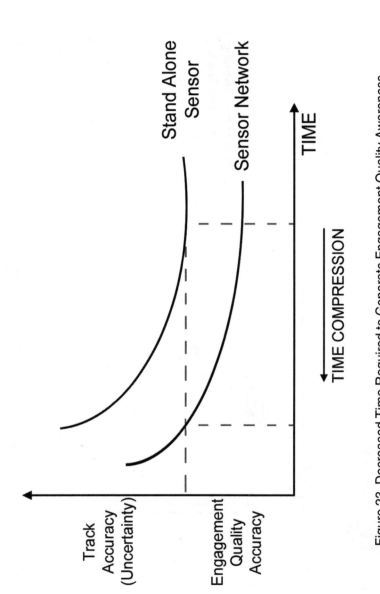

Figure 23. Decreased Time Required to Generate Engagement Quality Awareness

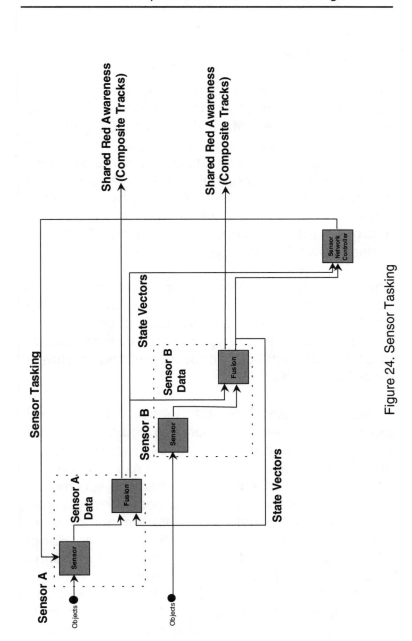

Figure 24. Sensor Tasking

tasking, can be quite significant, particularly against stressing targets.

The U.S. Navy's Cooperative Engagement Capability (CEC) provides proof of the existence of the power and operational benefits of NCW. The CEC generates increased battlespace awareness by fusing data from multiple sensors and enabling quantum improvements in track accuracy, continuity, and identification over the information that could be achieved by using stand-alone sensors. The performance in tracking improvement associated with the embedded CEC sensor network is portrayed in Figure 25.

The CEC, by also linking actor entities together, is able to exploit this improved information to increase combat power by extending the battlespace, enabling incoming targets to be engaged at greater ranges and in depth with multiple shooters yielding increased probability of kill.

Passive Sensors. The performance limits of stand-alone, passive sensors operating against objects in air and space can also be overcome through employment of sensor networks. For example, passive sensors, designed to detect and track objects moving in air and space (e.g., missiles, post-boost vehicles, re-entry vehicles, satellites, debris), can only measure azimuth and elevation (and rates) directly. Range information can be inferred but cannot be measured directly. Accurate tracking requires multiple observations (azimuth and elevation) to develop a track. Signature observables, such as plume intensity, are sometimes useful. In some cases, the proximity of an object to the earth (e.g., a missile in boost phase)

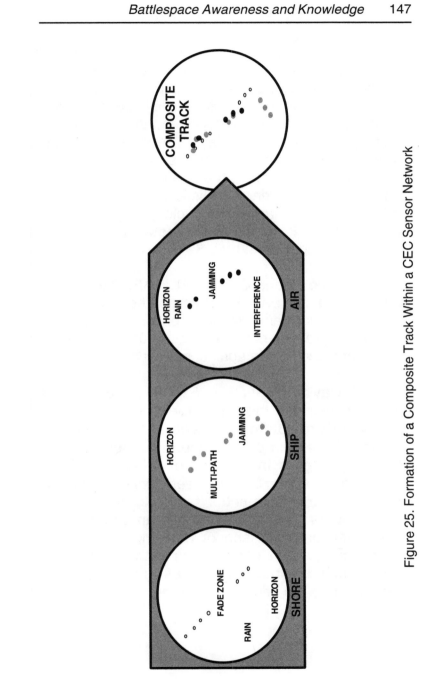

Figure 25. Formation of a Composite Track Within a CEC Sensor Network

can be exploited by a passive sensor to develop a more accurate track. The combination of sensor fusion and dynamic sensor tasking, made possible by linking sensors, can generate tracks on objects of interest that are significantly more accurate than those which can be generated by stand-alone sensors. Figure 26, Increased Battlespace Awareness Generated by a Sensor Network, portrays the operational benefit of a sensor network tracking a ballistic missile from launch until impact. The improved tracking accuracy of a sensor network is shown by the reduction in the size of the error ellipsoid vs. time.[72]

The Air Force Space Command's (AFSPACECOM) Attack and Launch Early Reporting to Theater (ALERT) capability provides an existence proof of the operational benefit of a sensor network in generating increased battlespace awareness against ballistic missiles.

The U.S. Navy's *Fleet Battle Experiment Series* has also demonstrated the ability for a sensor network consisting of ground- and sea-based radars to generate increased battlespace awareness against stressing targets in support of full-dimensional protection missions. During *Fleet Battle Experiment Delta*, land-based fire-finder radars and sea-based AEGIS radars were integrated into an experimental sensor network. This sensor network provided the ground component commander with significantly enhanced battlespace awareness to support the prosecution of the counter fire mission.

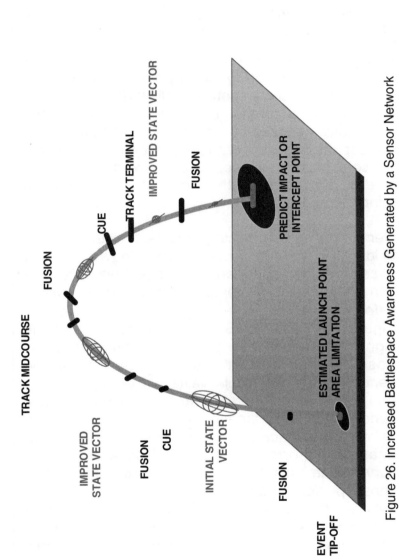

Figure 26. Increased Battlespace Awareness Generated by a Sensor Network

Application of Sensor Networks to the Surveillance and Tracking of Moving and Mobile Objects on the Surface of the Earth

Information about moving and mobile ground targets can also be improved by robustly networking sensors. Employment of sensor networks allows us to overcome line-of-sight obscuration by terrain, or environmental constraints imposed by weather. The combination of sensor tasking and data fusion enables multiple sensors, based in space, the air, or on the ground, to effectively increase the amount and quality of information available.

Certain classes of objects cannot be tracked, located, or identified with sufficient accuracy using a single type of sensor or sensor phenomenology. This deficiency can sometimes be overcome by linking sensors of different types to achieve an all source capability. Figure 27, Payoff of Sensor Fusion, portrays the significant reduction in position uncertainty that is possible with sensor fusion.[73] This increased performance is of particular value in detecting, locating, and identifying high-value targets, such as mobile surface-to-air or surface-to-surface missile launchers, as well as surface-to-surface missiles in flight. For example, information collected by a wide-area surveillance sensor, such as a radar MTI located on sensor platform such as a U-2 or an E-8 JSTARs, can be used to cue other sensor entities with different characteristics or capabilities such as imaging sensors, ELINT sensors, or manned reconnaissance teams. The operational concept of a multi-source sensor network was explored by the U.S. Marine Corps during the Hunter Warrior Advanced Warfighting Experiment

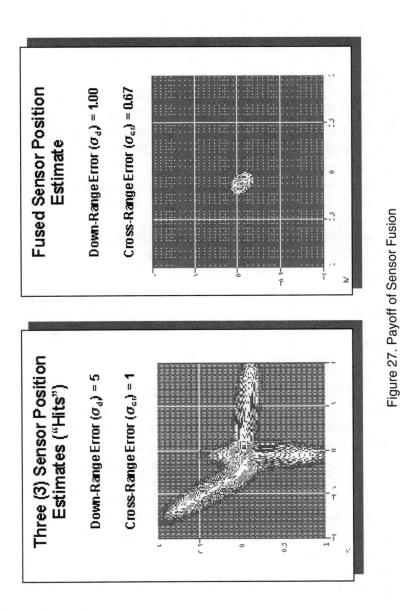

Figure 27. Payoff of Sensor Fusion

(AWE) in January 1997, and in Information Superiority Experiment (ISX) 1.1 in September 1998.

An example of the performance improvement of a sensor network against moving ground targets vs. a stand-alone sensor is portrayed in Figure 28, Performance Increase of Sensor Network Against Moving Ground Targets.[74] This figure highlights the degree to which the capability of a force to track and identify moving targets can be improved through the employment of a sensor network employing multiple types of sensors. In some cases, the capability to replay and review information that has been collected by sensors can have a significant operational payoff. This was the case during *Operation Desert Shield/ Desert Storm*, when information collected by the E-8 JSTARS was replayed and analyzed to locate forward operating bases that were being used by Iraqi forces.

Operational Capabilities of Mission Specific Sensor Networks

Sensor networks provide the warfighting force with the operational capability to synchronize battlespace awareness with military operations. In some mission areas, such as the Joint Suppression of Enemy Air Defenses and Joint Theater Air and Missile Defense, the capability to generate a very high level of battlespace awareness can have significant operational value. Consequently, commanders place a high value on generating this awareness. Mission-specific sensor networks provide commanders with the capability to task organize a broad spectrum of sensing capabilities to support the prosecution of the JSEAD and Air and Missile Defense missions. For

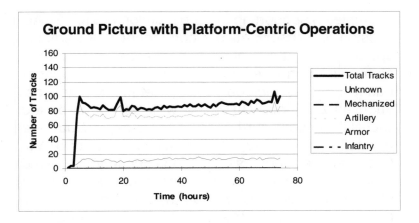

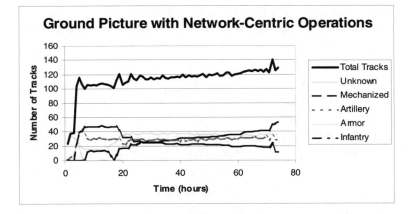

Figure 28. Performance Increase of Sensor
Network Against Moving Ground Targets

example, in supporting the prosecution of the JSEAD mission, a sensor network commander can employ space-, air-, and ground-based sensors to locate elements of an Enemy Air Defense System. Space-based sensors include missile detection satellites, such as DSP or SBIRS, as well as space-based SIGINT systems. Air-based sensors can include the E-8 JSTARS, the U-2, and the multiple types of UAVs. Ground-based sensors can include unattended ground systems, as well as special operations forces.[75] To effectively employ this broad range of sensors and to maximize their performance in support of the JSEAD mission, a sensor network commander needs to have the operational capability to maneuver, task, and prioritize the employment of sensors. This includes the capability to maneuver sensors, such as UAVs and JSTARS, to specific locations in the battlespace, as well as the capability to task sensor payloads in near real time. In some cases, this may require the ability to retask in real time a space-based sensor with a preplanned mission to collect information in support of battle damage assessment. Furthermore, real-time sensor data fusion requires that the information collected by these sensors be transported with near-zero time delay (a very high velocity of information) to high-performance data fusion nodes. Maintaining a high velocity of information between the elements of sensor network places a demand on the infostructure for dynamically prioritizing the transport and processing of information (Quality of Service).

In closing, we can see that the ability to significantly increase battlespace awareness and knowledge corresponds to a new core competency, a competency that is fundamental to achieving information superiority. As has been discussed in this chapter, developing this new core competency calls for new operational capabilities, such as the capability to deploy and operate sensor networks to ensure critical information availability. New concepts for network-centric operations, which integrate changes in technology, organization, and doctrine, are examples of new network-centric mission capability packages, a concept that will be discussed in detail in future chapters.

Command and Control and Execution

We have seen in the previous chapter how adopting NCW significantly increases our ability to generate shared battlespace awareness and to contribute to battlespace knowledge. In this chapter we address the implications of NCW for command and control and execution.

The very essence of command and control (C2) lies in the ability of a commander, at any level, to make the most out of the situation. In order to do so, commanders come equipped with the education, training, and experience that they bring to the situation, the assets and supplies they are assigned, and with access to information and decision support.

The output of a C2 process consists of the decisions a commander makes, the degree to which the commander's perception of the situation and the commander's intent is shared among the forces, and manifestations of command decisions (e.g., plans, orders, and information). In the final analysis, none of these C2 products will make any difference unless they are translated into effective actions in the battlespace. This is one reason this chapter addresses both C2 and execution. Another reason is the C2 and execution processes are, as a result of a shift towards network-centric operations, beginning to merge into a single, integrated process. This is driven by a need for an increased pace of operations and the need to improve responses in time-critical situations. Using network-centric concepts and enabling technologies, we can achieve a very high degree of coupling between C2 and fire control. This tight coupling enables us to translate high levels of shared battlespace awareness into increased combat power. Increased combat power can also be achieved in a number of other ways. These include collaborative planning and execution, reach back and split operations, and self-synchronized operations. Examples of these are presented later in this chapter.

NCW provides opportunities to improve both C2 and execution at each echelon in the context of particular missions and tasks. These opportunities will come about because:

1) decision entities or C2 elements will be more knowledgeable;
2) actor entities will be more knowledgeable;
3) actor and decision entities will be better connected;
4) sensor entities will be more responsive; and
5) the footprint of all entities will be much smaller.

Each of these improvements makes it possible for us to do things differently. It is important to stress that these properties of NCW offer opportunities to better match our approach to each set of battlespace circumstances and conditions to achieve greater levels of both effectiveness and efficiency.

Decision entities that are more knowledgeable will be able to approach problems in ways that less knowledgeable entities cannot. Decision-making processes no longer need focus on the defensive oriented approaches that were required to hedge against uncertainties (fog and friction). They can now focus instead on being proactive and agile. Increased levels of battlespace knowledge mean that we can accurately bound our adversary's capabilities. This allows us to devote more attention to shaping the battlespace and less to reacting to sudden or unexpected changes. Less energy will be spent on planning. The C2 and execution processes will become integrated as energies are devoted to contingency execution monitoring and real-time modification.

Knowledgeable actor entities will alter the approach to C2 from a process that embeds plans and decisions (making them detailed) to a process of conveying broad intent and orchestrating support of executing entities. With less detail being incorporated into orders, the speed of command can be greatly increased. The mechanics of C2 will be significantly reduced as the need to embed information in commands is reduced, contributing to increased command agility.

Better connectivity among actor and decision entities will result in an increased ability to react and effectively respond to changes in the situation. This agility will be greatly enhanced by having more responsive sensor entities. The ability to rapidly respond to changing circumstances has profound implications for C2 and related planning activities. It makes planning significantly easier as plans neither need to last as long, nor do they need to account for as many factors.

The ability to fine-tune operations will tend to make planning a continuous process that merges, under certain circumstances, with execution to the point where planning no longer remains a separate activity.

At any given level these changes will radically alter the nature of C2 by allowing us to push down more responsibility to what are now lower levels in the organization. Despite the resulting increased operating tempo, high-level decision entities will find themselves with more time and resources that can be concentrated on monitoring the situation and looking ahead to ensure that problems are identified and resolved as quickly as possible, perhaps even before the actor entities realize they exist.

NCW offers the opportunity not only to be able to develop and execute highly synchronized operations, but also to explore C2 approaches based upon horizontal coordination, or self-synchronization, of actor entities. In fact, the Marines have adopted *Command and Coordination* as their preferred term for command and control in future operations.[76]

This adds a whole new dimension to command and control. It recognizes that the behavior of an organization can be influenced and perhaps even controlled without the issuance of detailed top-down direction. It offers the alternative of achieving the desired results in another way. That is to say that organizational behavior could be consciously designed to be an emergent property that derives from the commander's intent, as internalized by actor entities, the degree of battlespace knowledge available and the ability of decision entities to minimize the constraints imposed on actor entities by virtue of the resources allocated to actor entities. It is hard to overestimate the impact that this new dimension of command and control will have on the way we will approach operations in the future.

The future battlespace, whether it involves large-scale, theater-size operations or situations in an urban environment, will be fast-paced and complex. It has always been the job of command and control to deal with the complexity of battle. NCW gives us important new tools to deal with this complexity. Until recently, it has been almost a fundamental article of faith that as we got more advanced technologically and organizationally, we would be able to tame complexity by insightful decomposition and massive amounts of processing power. We believed that if we could understand the underlying processes, we could handle any level of complexity by hard work and rigorous analysis, and with enough time and intellectual energy, we could develop the necessary levels of understanding to be successful.

There are scientists in many fields who are now expressing doubt about our traditional approach to very complex problems. They point out that many relatively simple processes cannot be adequately modeled, even with the vastly increased computer power we have recently developed.[77] They point out that system behaviors can become unpredictably unstable or chaotic.[78] Managing complex systems and situations in the absence of reliable predictive models is, of course, what command and control has always been about. NCW gives us more to work with to tame complexity and bound aberrant system behavior.

Exciting work is being done by the Marine Corps in their Combat Development Command to explore the characteristics and limits of emergent behaviors that result from various small unit/group rules of engagement and information environments.

NCW gives us the opportunity to explore the vast middle ground between the Industrial Age top-down hierarchical command and control approach and the highly decentralized model of small units assigned pieces of the problem with only their organic capabilities. This vast middle allows us to consider a host of command and control approaches, many of which could be used simultaneously in the battlespace of the future, each optimized for a specific task or function. The overall design of command and control, the way each mission, function, and task will be managed, needs to be conceived in such a way as to bound the overall behavior of the forces. In other words, the goal of command and control—to achieve high levels of force effectiveness and efficiency—needs to be achieved within acceptable levels of risk.

There are different kinds of risk that need to be considered. Added to the risks that commanders have dealt with for centuries are the risks of non-linear effects that come with the increased complexity of the battlespace of the future. A non-linear effect is one that is grossly disproportionate to the change in the independent variable(s). If an organization or system is behaving in a well-mannered or linear fashion, a small change in conditions (inputs or independent variables) will result in a small change in the result (output or dependent variable). A non-linear system or a system with discontinuities will exhibit large changes in behavior given small changes in initial conditions.

To the extent we currently understand the conditions under which this happens in battle, a different set of conditions is what we'll experience in the future. In large part our current approach to command and control is designed to reduce the chances that we will fall victim to these non-linear effects. Our current approach to C2 is designed to minimize mistakes and place bandages on potential weaknesses. However, this approach does not translate well into the Information Age, for it is based on limited information flows and restricted initiative, and is an approach that requires (or at least desires) overwhelming force. At times we have adapted approaches that have reduced operating tempo to achieve this objective. Our command and control challenge is to eliminate (or significantly reduce) the risks that accompany non-linear behavior or, if possible, put ourselves in a position to exploit the anomalies in an environment where the operating tempo, information flow, and initiative are increased.

Speed of Command

A basic measure of one's command and control approach, organization, and systems is speed of command, or the time it takes to recognize and understand a situation (or change in the situation), identify and assess options, select an appropriate course of action, and translate it into actionable orders. As long as the appropriate course of action is within the framework of the current plan, the plan survives. Replanning is a time consuming and manpower intensive activity during which combat effectiveness is, by definition, not what it could be. Recognizing that there is a problem or opportunity is the first step in this process.

In platform-centric military operations, situational awareness steadily deteriorates. Periodically, it is reestablished, and then it deteriorates again. Consequently, one reason no plan survives initial contact with the enemy is because situational awareness doesn't. Low levels of awareness slow down the planning process, as commanders delay decisions until key elements of information are updated.

The effect that network-centric operations can have on the speed of command was illustrated during the Taiwan Straits crisis in 1995, when the People's Republic of China attempted to influence Taiwanese elections with some highly visible saber rattling. This potentially explosive situation was defused when the United States quickly maneuvered two carrier battle groups into the Taiwan Straits. For our purposes, the most exciting part of that story was the fundamentally different way that command and control was exercised. The nature of Admiralty changed when then Vice Admiral Clemins, as Commander, Seventh Fleet, and his subordinates reduced their planning timelines from days to hours. This magnitude of change suggests that something very fundamental changed.

Admiral Clemins was able to use e-mail, a very rich graphic environment, and video teleconferencing to create and maintain a high level of shared awareness, and use this shared awareness to plan collaboratively. This significantly accelerated the process of synchronizing the operations of two carrier battle groups.[79]

At the tactical level, the U.S. Navy's *Fleet Battle Experiment Series* has demonstrated that combat power can be significantly increased through the ability of tactical units to self-synchronize operations based on a shared combat operational picture and shared knowledge of commander's intent. The self-synchronization that occurred was enabled through employment of a land-sea engagement network.

At what we currently refer to as the operational level of war, emerging Joint and Service doctrine and future warfighting concepts address the imperative for accelerating the pace of movement of forces, maintaining an unrelenting operational tempo, and decisively engaging the enemy and impacting events at the time and place of our choosing.[80] The emerging warfighting calculus asserts the potential of shock and awe to dislocate and confuse an enemy to the point that his warfighting structures quickly disintegrate and his feasible courses of action are rapidly reduced. The anticipated result is an unequivocal military decision with minimum cost to both sides.

Closely associated with these ideas is the concept of strategic lockout. Lockout refers to the situation that exists when an adversary's strategic objectives have been locked out because he has no remaining viable courses of action. This relationship is portrayed in Figure 29. Although the hypothesis is still unproven, the underlying logic is that focusing on strategic lockout can play a key role to enable a warfighting force to achieve a rapid termination of hostilities.

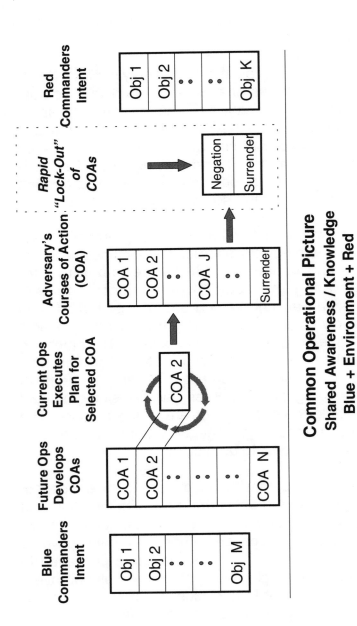

Figure 29. Lockout

Rehearsal

High fidelity rehearsals can achieve significant increases in combat effectiveness. By exploiting the infostructure that enables network-centric operations, warfighters can access sophisticated mission planning tools and simulators. Given the ability to repeatedly rehearse and analyze a given mission with the latest information available, a warfighter can improve the plan, develop enhanced awareness, and as a result, increase the probability of a successful outcome.

Engagement with Enhanced Awareness

Currently, computer-based software applications (e.g., Air Force Mission Support System (AFMSS), PowerScene, and TopScene) enable warfighters to generate an enhanced awareness of the battlespace by first planning and then rehearsing missions through photo-realistic visualization of a battlespace using 3-D scene visualization (virtual reality).

For example, a pilot can rehearse a mission several times and generate an increased awareness of the ingress route, engagement zone, and egress route. Threat characteristics, such as radar detection zones and surface-to-air missile (SAM) engagement zones can be represented in 3-D, enabling a pilot to plan and rehearse missions that minimize the probability of detection and engagement by enemy air defense systems. This increased awareness increases survivability by enabling a pilot to select a route that exploits terrain masking and or presents a reduced signature to known air defense radars. Furthermore, mission rehearsal can enable a pilot to increase the probability of target acquisition by identifying an attack profile that maximizes target acquisition under various light or weather conditions. Mission rehearsal can also help a pilot identify situations where mission planners have provided potentially incorrect target coordinates.

Each of these examples was played out in *Operation Deliberate Force* in Bosnia (August-September 1995) when NATO aircrews flew 3,515 sorties of which over 60 percent were flown by shooters. The value of enhanced battlespace awareness was manifested in the form of increased precision and lethality, reduced collateral damage, and minimal losses. Aircrews successfully attacked over 97 percent of the targets and destroyed or inflicted serious damage on more than 80 percent of them. The target set, which consisted of over 338 aim points within 48 complexes, was painstakingly selected, checked, and rechecked to virtually eliminate the risk to civilian life and property. During the entire operation, only a single aircraft, a French Mirage 2000K, was shot down. The crew survived and was eventually repatriated.[81] The value that emerged as a result of precision engagement was clearly a function of timely and accurate information, such as information on the status and disposition of adversary forces, as well as detailed environmental information.

Execution

We have seen how employing NCW provides us an opportunity to increase battlespace awareness and knowledge, to develop new approaches to command and control, and to more dynamically plan and rehearse missions. In the final analysis, this will not make much difference if we cannot translate these improvements into more effective and efficient execution.

Actor entities will have greatly increased access to information and expertise as was explained earlier in the example from the *Power of NCW* section. In addition, actor entities will be better able to communicate with all other battlespace entities. This is not of itself necessarily good, but if we do it right, an actor's increased knowledge of the battlespace and connectivity certainly could be profitably exploited.

Let us assume for a moment that the physical capabilities of our weapons systems remain essentially the same for the near-term future. This is not an unreasonable assumption, given the time it takes to conceive, develop, and deploy major weapons systems. Making this assumption allows us to place a lower bound on the value of NCW. However valuable we determine NCW to be in this restricted near term, it would be a tragic mistake to not pursue vigorous efforts aimed at the conceptualization and development of new weapons capabilities that allow us to better leverage the characteristics inherent in NCW. In other words, our first order of business is to see how we can make better use of our current weapons systems inventory using the concepts that are embedded in NCW.

Associated with the employment of actor entities are certain characteristics that determine their effectiveness and efficiency. Included are:

1) the targets they can engage or their engagement envelope;

2) their exposure to enemy attacks or their risk profile;
3) the speed of command and rate of engagement they can sustain (or their tempo);[82]
4) the responsiveness of forces or support units;
5) their ability to move (or their maneuverability);
6) their lethality (or the probability of kill); and
7) the extent to which their activities can be synchronized.

Adoption of NCW provides us with the ability to enlarge the engagement envelope, reduce risk profiles, increase operating tempo and responsiveness, improve maneuverability, and achieve higher kill probabilities.[83] A number of examples follow which illustrate these points.

Cooperative Engagement

Examples of enlarging the engagement envelope, increasing tempo, and reducing risk profiles can all be found in the Navy's Cooperative Engagement Capability.

The Cooperative Engagement Capability (CEC) improves our ability to conduct Air Defense. In this mission area, time is a key factor since there is a limited amount of time available to detect, track, classify, and engage targets. Engagement time is further compressed for high-speed or low-observable targets. This stresses all elements of the combat power value chain: sensors, command and control, and weapons.

CEC increases combat power by changing the relationships between battlespace and battletime. The CEC component forces currently consist of surface combatants (e.g., AEGIS Cruisers) and early warning aircraft (e.g., E-2 Hawkeye). Concepts will emerge enabling other elements, such as fighter aircraft, and ground-based missiles (e.g., Patriot Missiles or Hawk Missiles) to be employed as part of the CEC, serving to further increase combat power.

The CEC is enabled by the close coupling of an integrated communications capability in the form of the Data Distribution System (DDS), with a computational capability, in the form of the Cooperative Engagement Processor (CEP). This infostructure provides a high performance backplane which is key to increasing the velocity of information among sensor, C2, and fire control nodes. The netting of sensors generates a level of battlespace awareness that far surpasses that which could be generated by sensors operating in stand-alone mode. Shared engagement quality information is provided directly to the cognizant air defense commander, as well as to all other warfighters that have access to the CEC infostructure.

The actor entities that are linked to the CEC infostructure give the air defense commander the capability to employ forces in multiple modes. In the first mode, the netting of command and control and fire control capabilities provides the commander with automated decision support capabilities that help him identify the locations and weapons status of linked shooters. This information is combined with other battlespace information to identify the shooters that can engage each incoming target. The commander is then able to make effective force employment decisions: when to engage each target and what weapon to engage with. In this mode, the commander has centralized operational control over all connected weapons systems. Because of the short timelines involved, and the large number of decisions that potentially need to be made, a second mode has been created which automates the weapon target assignment process.

The value added by the CEC is a result of its ability to extend the engagement envelope, enabling incoming targets to be engaged in depth with multiple shooters with increased probability of kill. Furthermore, the inherent capability to engage adversary missiles by aircraft using engagement quality information generated by sensors not organic to the ship can increase the survivability of the ship by enabling it to engage without generating an electrical signature. The net result is the ability of the CEC to successfully engage and defeat threats capable of defeating a platform-centric defense. The whole is clearly greater than the sum of the parts.[84]

Beyond Line of Sight Engagement

Another example of extending the engagement envelope involves enabling forces to engage beyond their line of sight. A necessary condition for engaging targets without organic sensors or beyond line of sight of organic sensors is for engagement quality information to be generated externally and made available to the weapon or weapons system.

Engagement quality information consists of adequate position/velocity and identification to discriminate among blue forces, adversary forces, and neutrals in the engagement zone. This provides the commander and his forces with the information required to select a weapon with an acceptable probability of hard kill or soft kill and to employ the weapon with confidence that friendly forces are not within the effective range of the weapon during fly out or impact. Applying this to Joint operations will enable a Joint force to exploit the availability of engagement quality information to precisely engage adversary forces across the depth and breadth of the battlespace with a wide spectrum of beyond line of sight weapons (TACMS, TLAM, Enhanced Range Guns). Embedded C2 capabilities for near real time threat assessment, closure prediction, and distributed weapon-target assignment will enable the commander to synchronize employment of ground, air, and naval fires employing beyond line of sight munitions to perform anticipatory interdiction, and increase attrition of adversary forces prior to contact with ground forces.

Massing of Effects

The application of NCW to the Suppression of Enemy Air Defense (SEAD) mission provides an illustration of reduction of risk profiles and increases the probability of target kills. Figure 30 portrays the results of an analysis of SEAD.[85] In this analysis, the High-Speed Anti-Radiation Missile (HARM) Block 6 is used to suppress or destroy enemy Surface-to-Air Missile (SAM) sites, in some cases in conjunction with other shooters.

When we employ platform-centric operations (*Option 1*) during this particular scenario, we achieve virtually no kills. The HARM will still suppress the SAM sites because site operators realize that these missiles are out there, so they adjust their behavior. This is powerful in itself, but those SAM sites stayed there throughout the duration of the scenario. Consequently, aircraft that carry HARM missiles had to fly throughout the duration of the campaign, and all strike aircraft continued to be at risk. With *Option 2*, we are able to network sensors and shooters, resulting in an improved ability to generate and exploit battlespace awareness.

By employing NCW we can bring to bear other shooters capable of attacking SAM sites, such as tactical missiles (*Option 3*). The addition of this shooter capability, which requires changes in organization and doctrine, allows us to destroy virtually all of the SAM sites during the scenario. It is easy to focus on the extreme right-hand part of the curves, depicted in Figure 30, but the payoff is on the left where a very high rate of change is developed. When 50 percent of something important to an adversary is destroyed at the outset, so is his strategy. That stops wars. This is precisely what Network Centric Warfare seeks to do, and that is what lockout is all about.[86]

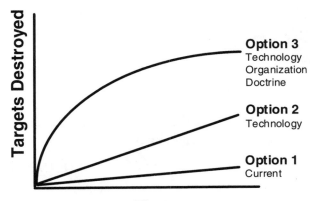

OPTION 1	**Current Shooter Grid Awareness +** **HARM BLK 6**
OPTION 2	**Improved Shooter Grid Awareness +** **HARM BLK 6** (Technology)
OPTION 3	**Improved Shooter Grid Awareness +** **HARM BLK 6 + ATACMS** (Technology / Organization / Doctrine)

Figure 30. JSEAD Mission Effectiveness

Self-Synchronization

Self-synchronization is perhaps the ultimate in achieving increased tempo and responsiveness. Self-synchronization is a mode of interaction between two or more entities. Figure 31 portrays the key elements of self-synchronization: two or more robustly networked entities, shared awareness, a rule set, and a value-adding interaction. The combination of a rule set and shared awareness enables the entities to operate in the absence of traditional hierarchical

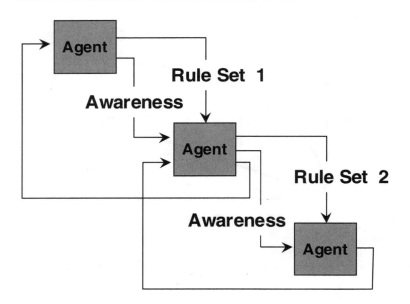

Figure 31. Self-Synchronization Interaction

mechanisms for command and control. The rule set describes the desired outcome in various operational situations. Shared awareness provides a mechanism for communicating the ongoing dynamics of the operational situation and triggering the desired value-adding interaction.

Self-synchronization can take many forms in the warfighting ecosystem. There are certain types and kinds of relationships that by their nature do not lend themselves to self-synchronization and others where the application of self-synchronization can yield significant benefits. An area where the application of self-synchronization has significant potential is a class of warfighting activities providing supporting services, such as logistics, fire support, and close air support. In platform-centric operations, the supported agent typically requests support, often via voice. Significant time is often spent communicating position information. In many cases, there are multiple distractions that complicate the exchange of information. However, as the level of shared battlespace awareness increases, new types of relationships are possible.

When the value-adding interaction takes the form of logistical support, self-synchronization provides a mechanism for pushing logistics in anticipation of need. For example, one can easily envision a situation in ground operations where near real time information on consumption of fuel and ammunition in weapons platforms (e.g., M1A2 Tanks, M2 Bradley Fighting Vehicles) combined with an agreed-to rule set could significantly improve logistical support. In fact, information on fuel consumption and ordnance expenditure is currently collected in real time with sensors embedded in F-18 aircraft. This awareness information is transmitted in real time via Link 4A to C2 and the Carrier Air Operations cell. This real time awareness enables the operational commander to redirect aircraft with fuel and ordnance to secondary targets as required. Furthermore, information on fuel consumption can be used by Air Operations to prioritize and readjust the landing queue in real time based on fuel remaining. In addition, aircraft maintainers are able to preposition required ordnance to enable rapid re-arming of aircraft. This has proven to have significant operational benefit, because ordnance needs to be moved from the ship's magazines, which takes time.

Another example of experimentation with self-synchronization comes from the U.S. Army. Recent experiences at Fort Hood, Texas, point to numerous examples where more emphasis was placed upon the use of commander's intent and where units were permitted more freedom of action to explore the ability of low-level forces (platoon and company) to operate near autonomously by retasking themselves. Warfighter exercises at both division and corps levels also indicate an increasing interest in exploring self-synchronizing forces.[87]

The most recent proof of the enormous potential of self-synchronization was provided by *Fleet Battle Experiment* (FBE) *Delta*, conducted in October 1998 in conjunction with *Exercise Foal Eagle '98*. This is an annual Joint and combined exercise sponsored by Combined Forces Command, Korea. The experiment used both real and simulated forces. The focus of *Exercise Foal Eagle* was on countering a North Korean artillery and rocket attack on Seoul and other allied positions, countering North Korean special operations forces, and improving Joint theater air and missile defense. The network-centric concepts experimented within FBE Delta linked Army and Navy sensors and shooters in ways that had not previously been considered. The result of the employment of these network-centric concepts was the generation of a very high level of shared battlespace awareness, which was exploited to increase combat power.

For example, in the Counter SOF Mission, the seemingly intractable problem of countering hundreds of North Korean special operations boats was dealt with on a timeline previously not thought possible. The application of network-centric concepts enabled Army helicopters, P-3s, LAMPS, AC-130s, and land- and carrier-based aircraft units to share a common operational picture and to synchronize their efforts from the bottom up. This self-synchronization demonstrated the capability for leakers to be reduced by an order of magnitude and for the operational mission to be accomplished in half the time required, compared to traditional platform-centric operations. Figure 32 demonstrates the significantly increased combat power that can be generated with network-centric operations.

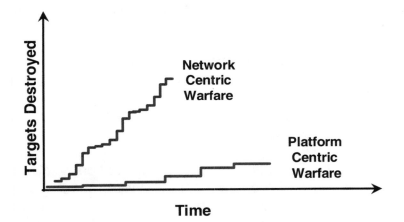

Figure 32. Network Centric Warfare—
Fleet Battle Experiment Delta

The operational impact of this significantly increased combat power at the tactical level is that forces that otherwise would have needed to be held in reserve to deal with leakers (SOF forces that penetrate the defensive forces) can now be reassigned, changing the complexion of the battle. This is an example of the potential for network-centric operations at the tactical level to have operational and strategic implications.

When reduced to these elementary terms, it sounds so simple, but it had never been done before and the impact was profound. This seems to characterize all great advances.[88]

Tempo and Responsiveness

Short of self-synchronization, there are a variety of ways to achieve less dramatic, but meaningful increases in tempo and responsiveness. Increasing tempo and responsiveness both involve reducing timelines while maintaining or increasing quality. These could involve reducing the:

1) time between target detection and delivery of munitions on target;
2) time to plan; or
3) time necessary to form and equip forces to conduct operations.

Figure 33, Operational Gains of Digitization,[89] shows the nature of the operational impact of reducing the time it takes to plan, respond to a call for fire, mount an attack, and move to contact. The U.S. Army's Division XXI AWE produced dramatic results by killing over twice the enemy in half the time at over three times the battlespace with 25 percent fewer combat platforms using Information Age technology.[90]
The examples that follow illustrate the value of increased tempo and/or responsiveness in three situations: fire support, engagement, and logistics.

Providing fire support involves responding to requests for fire, forwarded by multiple warfighters dispersed across the battlespace, given a finite set of weapons

Activity (Before/After)	OPTEMPO	Lethality	Survivability
Plan Development (Div) 72 v 12 hrs	☑		
Call for Fire 3 v 0.5 min		☑	
Deliberate Attack (Co) 40 v 20 min	☑	☑	☑
Hasty Attack (Co) 39 v 112 Red Loss	☑	☑	
Defense in Sector Loss v Win		☑	☑
Movement to Contact 91 v 128 Red Loss		☑	☑

Figure 33. Operational Gains of Digitization

which are (most likely) also dispersed geographically across the batttlespace. Multiple factors conspire to complicate and potentially slow down the command and control process and reduce responsiveness to these urgent requests. These factors include simultaneous requests for fire, requests for fire that exceed available resources and the dynamic nature of the requests, and the capabilities (range, firing rate) of shooting assets. In approaching this problem, a value can be assigned to each call for fire, corresponding to the value of engaging the target by time T_{max} beyond which the value is dramatically reduced. The value assigned can be negative, which would correspond to blue losses that could result from supporting fires not being provided by time T_{max}.

Providing responsive fires requires that a set of weapon-target assignment decisions be made. Over a discrete time horizon (which is variable) the C2 node attempts to maximize the overall value of responding to calls for fire, while simultaneously minimizing the cost (e.g., why use a tactical missile if gun fire will do?) and potentially considering conserving fires (e.g., may or may not want to fire all tactical missiles in the first 30 minutes of battle; may want to if they are being used to take out high-value assets such as enemy air defense installations).

As the number of simultaneous calls for fire and the number of potential shooters and types of weapons increase, the target assignment problem becomes more difficult. Beyond some threshold, a human decision maker is overwhelmed, resulting in sub-optimal assignments, or worse, unacceptable delays in allocating fires (an example of value subtracting C2).

Consequently, the use of automated or semi-automated decision aides for weapon target assignments, robustly networking sensors, C2 nodes, and shooters, can increase combat power. The U.S. Navy in the Fleet Battle Experiment Series is exploring this concept. During *Fleet Battle Experiment Alpha*, an experimental concept, referred to as a *ring of fire* was employed. The ring-of-fire concept explores the potential for a robustly networked force of sea- and air-based shooters employing automated pairing of weapons to targets, automated force-wide weapons inventory, and integrated airspace deconfliction. These emerging capabilities will help sea-based shooters increase lethality against both time-critical targets and moving targets.

Another example of achieving improved responsiveness involves en route mission updates and/or target assignments enabled by a robust network that links shooters to C2 nodes. This concept was explored by the U.S. Air Force in *Expeditionary Force Experiment '98* (EFX '98) by launching a B-1B bomber into a broad engagement zone without specific targets, and then providing the B-1B with en route targeting and weaponeering information via tactical data links. This approach provides more flexibility and increased responsiveness (and perhaps improved lethality) by allowing the C2 node to include targets that may not have been detected and identified prior to takeoff and by providing more up-to-date location information by allowing the C2 node to choose targets based upon a more current assessment of the situation.[91]

The JV2010 concept of Focused Logistics aims at providing support that is more responsive and timely. A new operational capability serves to illustrate what lies ahead. To manifest 200 soldiers for air transport can take over 8 hours employing traditional techniques. During *Exercise Cobra Gold '98*, the use of smart-card technology and portable sensors enabled 200 soldiers to be manifested in 2 hours while the manifest information was loaded directly into the Global Transportation Network (GTN). Additional process changes have the potential to reduce the total manifest time to under an hour.[92] The result is both accelerated deployment of troops and material and increased in-transit visibility that serves to allow a commander to respond more quickly and increase tempo to the limit allowed by the logistics situation.

Implications

The effects of a series of improvements, such as illustrated above, are highly synergistic, making the resulting force much more effective and efficient. In fact, this synergy allows NCW, for the first time, to provide us with the possibility of moving beyond a strategy based upon attrition, to one based upon shock and awe.[93] Shock and awe are achieved not simply as a function of the number of targets destroyed, but as a result of the destruction or neutralization of significant numbers of critical targets within a short period of time and/or the successful targeting of the right target at the right time.

The key to this fundamental transformation from attrition to shock and awe lies in the increased ability to integrate. Integration must take place in a number of different dimensions if we are to be successful in realizing the potential benefits inherent in NCW. While increased connectivity enables this integration to take place, it remains only a potential capability until we develop operational concepts, command approaches, organizations, and the like that specify the processes that serve to integrate our tasks and activities over echelons, over time, functionally and geographically.

The engagement envelope for a particular actor is often constrained more by limits on engagement quality data and by existing doctrine about what targets (type and location) may be engaged, than by the range of the available weapons. Both of these artificial[94] constraints can be eliminated with the adoption of NCW.

Being in harm's way is not always intentional. Actors may find themselves placed in harm's way because of a lack of battlespace knowledge, maneuverability, or covering fire. In fact, it has often been the case that actors were placed in harm's way simply to gain information about the battlespace. For example, during the Cold War, U.S. Navy submarines were sent in harm's way to collect intelligence on the capabilities of Soviet Naval Forces.[95] Given the potentially significant increases in battlespace knowledge and engagement envelopes, and improvements in maneuverability that result from the adoption of NCW, actors will find themselves in harm's way only when it is absolutely essential to complete the task at hand. When placed in harm's way, NCW will provide them with an increased ability to be protected and/or removed from danger.

The ability to move depends, in large part, upon the size of the actor entity which, in many cases, can be reduced significantly by NCW-related concepts of reach-back and just-in-time logistics support.

Tempo, the pace of operational activity of forces in the battlespace, speaks to the intensity of the engagement and how rapidly the proper targets can be engaged. This is, of course, key to achieving shock and awe. The current cyclic nature of command and control limits decision throughput, and the separation of planning from execution limits tempo. Current limitations in the engagement envelope limit maneuvers. The ability to be better integrated over echelons, over time and functionally, is the key to achieving a much higher tempo, particularly given the expected increases in engagement ranges and the improvements in maneuverability. Achieving better integration over echelons will reduce the time it takes to transform a change in commander's intent into action or to implement a decision. The move from a cyclic C2 process that performs planning and execution sequentially and is characterized by a period to a more continuous process that merges planning and execution, will result in our ability to generate much higher tempos. Finally, the greater empowerment of actors will increase the decision-making resources available, allowing us to take advantage of parallel processing, and hence reduce or eliminate yet another factor that limits tempo.

Kill probability can be improved by obtaining more accurate information about targets and better matching weapons and targets. NCW approach helps us in a number of ways by being able to move quickly, getting the right information to the right place, and allowing us to have a wider selection in our assignment of a weapon to a particular target.

NCW offers a promising opportunity to both improve the effectiveness of military operations and to reduce their costs (measured in terms such as number of casualties, collateral damage, and strategic fallout). It promises to raise the art of war to new heights and enables us to compress military campaigns into time frames to be more consistent with our 21st century world.

The Entry Fee

The entry fee for Network Centric Warfare is an infostructure that provides all elements of the warfighting enterprise with access to high-quality information services.[96] What separates the future from the present will be the provision of nearly ubiquitous information services to all elements of the warfighting enterprise. These elements include deployed U.S. forces, supporting forces based in the United States, and allied and coalition partners. The required quality of service will vary as a function of the demands of each MCP across the enterprise as portrayed in Figure 34.[97]

At the high end of the performance spectrum is cooperative sensing and engagement of high-speed targets. Accomplishing this requires high data rate and very low latency information transport capabilities. At the intermediate level are various types of command and control activities, such as coordination of tactical combat operations, which can tolerate information delays on the order of seconds. These operations are typically supported by tactical data links. Other types of command and control and logistical operations, such as operational planning, are not nearly so time sensitive. For example, information about the contents of a large container ship, which may take tens of days to transit from a point of embarkation to debarkation, most likely can tolerate delays on the order of minutes. Similarly, the wide variation in the importance and

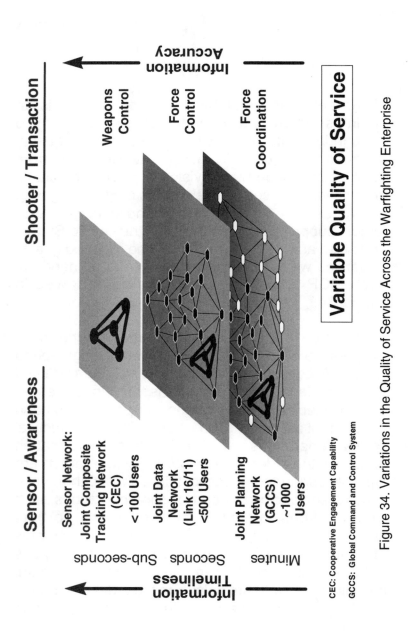

Figure 34. Variations in the Quality of Service Across the Warfighting Enterprise

urgency of e-mail traffic lends itself to various levels of latency and precedence.

There is a direct relationship between the velocity of information and the speed and tempo of operations across the warfighting enterprise. In the previous sections, we have seen that one of the primary motivations for providing high-quality information services to the warfighting force is to be able to achieve a large increase in the speed and tempo of operations. Such an increase is a prerequisite for many of NCW-based concepts of operations under discussion.

At a high level of abstraction, we can view the infostructure as an integrated network of communications and computational capabilities. The computational nodes and the communications links convey the seamless integration of computing and communications into a single *backplane*.

Our warfighting backplane will employ multi-mode data transport capabilities, including military and commercial satellite communications capabilities, multiple types of data links and radios, and commercial information services. These data transport capabilities will both provide users with access to appropriate elements of a distributed computing environment, as well as providing the interconnecting fabric for a wide range of computational and storage capabilities. The backplane supporting the infostructure will employ a multi-tiered architecture for information transport and processing to increase capacity and improve interoperability. By exploiting emerging technology for providing quality of service across Internet protocol

(IP)-based networks, the architecture of the infostructure will enable multiple stand-alone networks to be integrated into an adaptive and reconfigurable network-of-networks.[98] This operational flexibility will enable commanders to plug and play sensors, shooters, command and control, and support capabilities into task-organized combat packages, including appropriate collections of sensors and weapons.

A core technical capability for enabling variable quality of service information services and effectively exploiting finite information transport and processing capabilities is transaction-based prioritization of information transport and processing. In the current environment, several types and kinds of independent voice, video, and data networks (e.g., Defense Information Infrastructure, Tactical Digital Information Links) operate as independent networks for multiple reasons. One of the primary drivers for separate networks is the need to meet required timelines for information exchange. As was described previously, this is the situation that exists today, where tactical data links, such as Link 16 and CEC, operate with protocols which are separate and distinct from the protocols employed with Transmission Control Protocol/ Internet Protocol (TCP/IP)-based networks, such as the Secret Internet Protocol Router Network (SIPRNET). One of the primary drivers for separate networks is that until recently, IP networking technology could not enable quality of service to be linked to transaction type. The technology now exists to solve this problem.[99] In other cases, security requirements, combined with the limitations of existing technology, conspire to dictate separate networks, as is the case with the Sensitive but Unclassified Internet Protocol Router Network (NIPRNET) and the SIPRNET.

Since future warfare will rely heavily on increased connectivity among sensors, command nodes, and weapons, network security will be high priority. Integrated capabilities for information protection will provide the network-centric force with assured high-speed access to the information required to dominate across all levels of conflict. With the advent of information warfare techniques, it is no longer necessary for our adversaries to have direct physical access to our infostructure in order to attack us. We can be attacked from anywhere in the world, any time of the day or night. Enhancing the security and computer network defense capabilities of both the classified and unclassified elements of the infostructure will ensure that high-quality information services are available to the warfighter and supporting elements when and where they are needed.[100] An infostructure must be properly managed to ensure that it is dynamically tuned to meet the warfighter's needs. Enhanced capabilities for network operations will provide operational commanders with a real-time picture of the status of the backplane. This picture, when combined with advanced capabilities for intelligent network management, will provide commanders with the flexibility to tune the infostructure and synchronize information transport and processing with military operations.

Commercial information technology is driving the convergence of technologies for voice and data services. This technology will enable data traffic to be provided with the reliability and quality of service associated with dial tone, as well as new and exciting capabilities that we have not yet imagined. The technologies that emerge from the commercial sector, when augmented with specialized information technologies developed by the DoD, such as high-end encryption, low-probability of intercept and detection communications, and specialized intelligent agents, will provide the brick and mortar for our "Global Information Grid."[101]

The acquisition, deployment, and operation of the infostructure are and will continue to be an ongoing process. New and emerging technologies will continue to create exciting opportunities for both suppressing costs and improving performance. Integrating these technologies with existing systems and capabilities will be one of the most significant challenges we face as we move toward enabling a network-centric force. The next chapter is devoted to a discussion of each of the elements of an MCP, and the nature of the changes that will be required to be able to conduct network-centric operations.

Implications for MCPs

Innovation is inextricably tied to changing long-held precepts about the way we do things. Culture, rules, and tools determine how things get done. The concept of a mission capability package (MCP) is a useful way of describing and discussing a way of doing business. Multiple terms have been used throughout DoD to describe this basic concept. These include doctrine, organization, training, materiel, leadership, and personnel (DOTML-P) and doctrine, organization, materiel (DOM) (ACOM's characterization). An MCP consists of a concept of operations, command approach, organization, systems, and people with a prescribed level of expertise. Implicit in an MCP is the nature, distribution, and utilization of information. To make MCPs based upon NCW all that they can be, we need to rethink each and every component of an MCP. We will discuss the nature of the changes that will need to be made in each of an MCP's main components.

Concept of Operations

The process of building a new MCP begins with the development of the concept of operations (ConOps). In looking to see if a ConOps is really based on NCW, one needs to see if it takes full advantage of all the information and forces (sensor and actor entities) that could be available given the timeliness requirements of the mission. NCW-based ConOps should be focused on identifying and employing these entities in a manner that dominates the adversaries (or in the case of Humanitarian Assistance Operations, in a way that fully anticipates environmental factors) by determining the best time, places (targets), and methods (hard or soft) to intervene to achieve the desired end.

Command Approach

The command approach(es) selected or developed for the MCP should reflect the characteristics inherent in the ConOps. The nature of the command decisions to be made by battlespace entities, and those that are delegated to battlespace agents, need to reflect both distribution of battlespace knowledge over time and the time lines associated with the ConOps. In general, one would expect that in an NCW-based MCP, command decisions would migrate closer to the pointy end(s) of the spear. Ironically, this could at first glance seem to be coming full circle to the days when communications over any distances were very slow and limited, and local commanders acted almost autonomously. The major difference, of course, is that now an autonomous unit is really not truly autonomous because its behavior is heavily influenced by its view of the COP, and its perception of the commander's intent, even as they might change.

Organization

Form must follow function if NCW-based MCPs are to achieve their potential. The organizational form(s) designed by the MCP must be based upon the ConOps and Command Approach. Simply put, the organization should be designed to facilitate the flow of information and materials needed to carry out the tasks at hand. There should be no organizational barriers or speed bumps that degrade performance. NCW organizations therefore need to be *born joint* to ensure that all of the available information and assets can be brought to bear on the task at hand. It is anticipated that NCW-based organizational forms will be more agile than current ones. Perhaps operational organizations will become virtual ones, formed specifically to accomplish a particular set of tasks for just as long as necessary and then cease to be, with their resources going back into the mission infrastructure, waiting to be assigned once more. Depending upon the dynamics of the battlespace and the nature of the task at hand, these virtual organizations might exist for minutes or months.

Infostructure Systems

Infostructure systems will provide key capabilities (bandwidth, processing power, stored information, decision aids, and agents) and need to be better designed to support battlespace entities as they interact much more closely than ever before. The increased use of decision aids and battlespace agents will make it more important for the systems to be thoroughly tested before deployment. Just like organizations, their job is to enable and facilitate, not to get in the way. Legacy systems, designed as stove-pipes optimized for one way of doing business, will need to give way to systems that are optimized to share and exchange information (with appropriate security). Individual systems will no longer be effective unless they can contribute value as part of a larger federation of systems that constitute the infostructure.

NCW requires team play, not only among battlespace entities, but also from the systems and organizations that support them. Interoperability, security, and the teamwork they enable need to be part of the initial design of every system. They cannot be added later. Testing systems will become far more complex since the focus will not be on the performance of individual systems, but on the performance of federations of systems.

People

People are central to any MCP, for it is the people that turn concepts into realities and fill in the gaps and inconsistencies within and among organizations, systems, and battlespace knowledge. Collectively, people create and maintain culture, so in order to make NCW MCPs work, the force needs to be educated and trained to develop NCW attitudes and expertise. NCW doctrine needs to be written to support this process. NCW requires significant changes in mindset and much greater understanding of the information that is available and the processes, tools, and agents that turn this collection of information into battlespace knowledge. Individuals will need to know more about the battlespace and the roles of others in that battlespace. Doctrine will need to be developed and/or modified to emphasize the principles inherent in NCW, the new roles that battlespace entities will play, and the nature of their interactions. It will also be extremely important to give people an adequate opportunity to build trust in the information and tools that will be developed, and to develop a capability to absorb new and enhanced capabilities as they become available.

Coevolution of MCP

The process of engineering an MCP needs to encourage and facilitate the coevolution of its component parts right from the start. The melding of a ConOps, C2, organization, doctrine, weapons and infrastructure, systems, and personnel into a coherent MCP is essentially an interdisciplinary learning process that is one part discovery, one part testing, and one part practice. It could be said that teamwork is the co-pilot of NCW—from the conceptualization of new MCPs, to their refinement and demonstration, to the acquisition of needed components and the development of needed personnel, to their perfection through experience and practice.

Making NCW a Reality

Clearly, NCW has significant potential to transform our approach to assigned missions and achieve worthwhile improvements in effectiveness and efficiency. However, these gains will not be realized by simply putting an enabling infostructure in place. In fact, doing so without taking decisive steps to develop NCW-based mission capability packages could result in confusion and disharmonies, along with degraded performance and poor morale. Making NCW a reality requires that we first start with a clean sheet of paper and understand the implications for all of the elements or components of the force.

Two key prerequisites for success are in our control:

1) the development of new and innovative NCW concepts and strategies to meet mission challenges; and
2) the ability to transform these embryonic concepts and strategies into real operational capability, unconstrained by current institutional considerations.

What is needed to accomplish this are three linked processes—one designed to foster and incubate innovative ideas, one designed to introduce change, and a third process designed to insert technology. History is replete with examples of organizational failures to take timely advantage of the opportunities that advances in technology afford. These opportunity losses usually can be traced to a failure of (or lack of) one or more of these processes or the absence of the necessary links among them. History demonstrates that progress is eventually made, albeit at a much slower pace than was possible. Before the relatively recent explosion in the pace of technological advances, usually new technology was assimilated before it was itself obsolete. Technology is now advancing at a rate which far outpaces our ability to fully leverage its potential, and it is not uncommon to have organizations operating with technology that is more than one generation removed from the cutting edge. In fact, large organizations like DoD deploy at any given time technology from several different "generations." This only exacerbates problems with interoperability and security.

The Information Age is different, particularly for the military, than past eras in four fundamental ways that makes "business as usual" increasingly obsolete. First, the rate of technological advance, and the ability to turn out new products, has increased dramatically. Second, the advances in technology that are relevant for the military are, to a very large extent, no longer driven by known operational requirements.[102] Instead, they are being driven by private sector requirements to move and process information on a scale unimaginable just a few years ago. Third, the military is now being driven by a technology cycle that is quickening and has less and less time to react to take advantage of the new capabilities they represent before these, in turn, are overtaken by new capabilities. Fourth, the new capabilities are equally available to potential adversaries.

While much has been learned about putting technology to use, the pace of technological advances has quickened to such a degree that current DoD methods of incorporating technology are well behind the power curve. While reforms are underway to help reduce the time it takes to go from design to deployment, they alone will not be sufficient to bring about the changes needed to meet today's mission challenges. The reason is that the technology development cycle is out of sync with military strategy and doctrine development. Speeding up the technology cycle, without addressing the inertia in the processes by which we develop military strategy, concepts, and doctrine, just makes these processes more out of sync. What is needed is an approach that synchronizes the development of military strategy and doctrine with the advances in technology and with the technology insertion process.

The speed at which technology can be deployed is only one aspect of the problem. Consider a situation in which new technology can be made instantly available to operational users. How much of the technology's potential will be realized? At best, only incremental improvements will be made and only a small fraction of the potential utility of the technology will be realized. This is not to say that these incremental improvements would not be useful, or even important. But inescapably, a great deal of the potential of the technology would be unrealized. This scenario would be repeated over and over again as the latest technology replaced older technology. Thus, only a series of incremental changes and improvements in operational capability would be achieved.

What is needed is a set of tightly coupled processes that:

1) facilitates an understanding of emerging capabilities;
2) fosters innovative concepts;
3) expedites the testing and refinement of these concepts; and
4) focuses efforts on the development and deployment of coherent MCPs.

To achieve this we will need to adapt our existing requirements, investment planning, and programmatic processes, making them enterprise-wide in order to make NCW a reality in a timely fashion. Current practices bifurcate the requirements, funding, design, development, and acquisition processes for each of the elements of an MCP. Thus, rather than helping us coevolve, our culture and processes are doing just the opposite.

Lessons Learned

One can trace the origins of our current understanding of the need to coevolve MCPs to earlier work in evolution acquisition by the DoD and industry.[103] The rapid prototyping component of evolutionary acquisition[104] (EA) foreshadowed the current notion of coevolution. The concept of EA was developed as a result of widespread dissatisfaction with the results of systems acquisitions. More often than not, systems were delivered late, with significant cost overruns and worse of all, they failed to satisfy users even when they delivered the specified functionality. Before EA, systems were designed and acquired using a waterfall approach that moved sequentially from step to step, beginning by specifying the requirements in considerable detail. Once these requirements were specified and approved by the operational community, they were frozen, and developers went off to produce a system (taking a decade or so before it was returned as a fait accompli), and then finally it was turned over to the users (who of course were not the same ones who participated in the requirements phase). We, of course, know better now. But then systems were just beginning to be software dominated and the flexibility of software vis-à-vis hardware was not widely understood. But it is instructive to see what the developers of the EA approach identified as critical back then and note in their observations and recommendations the origins of our current philosophy of coevolution because it provides us with a better understanding of what will happen if we do not insist upon processes that will encourage and facilitate coevolution of MCPs.

Prior to EA, there was a commonly held belief that most of the problems incurred in systems development could be traced to poorly articulated requirements, and if only the users would just do a better job writing document requirements, everything would be fine. But the founders of EA recognized that users, no matter how hard they tried, were unable to specify in advance all of their requirements. This inability was not found to be caused by a lack of effort devoted to the requirements process, as was previously thought. Instead it was the result of a faulty assumption. It was believed that users know what their requirements are, or at least *should* know. In fact, it is unreasonable to expect users to know, in any detail, what their requirements are or will be, when they do not have a full appreciation of the new or improved technologies, particularly in terms of implications for the environment or mission.

Traditionally, users first saw technologies after they were packaged into deployable systems. Only after users gained experience with the new capabilities were they in a position to fully appreciate the possibilities in the context of their jobs. There are many problems associated with the dump-technology-on-the-users-and-run approach. First, the learning curve was often steep and it took some time before a significant portion of the new capabilities was actually employed. Second, only a fraction of the features contained in a system found their way into widespread use. Third, it was only after users started to appreciate the new technologies that they were able to think of ways they could be used. Let us look at each of these problems and see how EA was designed to remedy them so that we can incorporate these lessons learned into our approach to developing applications of NCW.

It turned out that the learning curve was more complex than originally thought. While much attention was focused on training users to operate the system to become familiar with the "knobs and switches," it soon became clear that command and control systems were not to be mastered simply by learning the user interface. In many cases the information contained in the system was significantly different from the information that was previously available. It may have been entirely new, a class of information that users only dreamed about having before, or sometimes information they never even knew existed. It may have been the same information except that it was now more timely or accurate. The information characteristics may not have changed, but the way information is presented could change. Finally, it may have been new analytical capabilities that took available information and added value to it.

In these cases, learning the system involved much more than learning the user interface. It took (and takes) time and lots of on-the-job practice. And the learning did not end there. Once a new capability was mastered and confidence was developed in its reliability, users started to see the possibilities. And these possibilities involved learning curves of their own. In fact, this was the hidden set of learning curves that EA brought out into the light. These "extra" learning curves were, in fact, users learning their new requirements. In retrospect, it seems ludicrous to have thought users could capture their requirements in a document without ever having been exposed to a hands-on version of the system in question, or without a chance to use the system in an operational context.

As a result of this improved understanding of the extent of learning that needs to take place, the EA approach scrapped the lengthy and unproductive paper requirements process and replaced it with the use of rapid prototypes, or simulations, that give users an approximation of hands-on experience. It uses the statement of requirements that is implicit in the iteratively developed prototype as the true expression of requirements. The EA approach speeds up the learning curve and matures the requirements more rapidly than before.

This lesson, once learned, needs to be relearned. In most if not all of the experiments to date, there simply has not been enough time provided to allow users to learn what the new systems could do and as a result the experiments are not as productive as they could be otherwise.[105]

The second problem with the traditional approach was that only a fraction of the systems capabilities was ever fully used. The causes for this vary widely. They include:

1) poorly conceived and/or executed requirements;
2) potentially very useful capabilities that cannot reach their potential because of constraints imposed by doctrine or organization;
3) capabilities that require more training to understand and employ; and
4) a lack of user trust or confidence in the system.

Replacing the paper requirements process with an iterative, hands-on approach also helps to address some of the root causes for failures to use system capabilities, but is inadequate in addressing the existence of self-imposed constraints. The full recognition of this problem, and the development of an approach to deal with it, was not fully articulated until the development of the MCP approach and with it the recognition of the need for coevolution. While an improved requirements process alone can make a significant difference, other aspects of EA serve to reinforce it and improve the probability that a system's capabilities will be useful when delivered. The notion of not biting off the whole job at once, but rather developing a set of core capabilities as an initial deployable delivery, aids the cause by reducing the amount of learning that users need to do and the change they need to assimilate. It makes it easier to move up the learning curve and reach a level of improved productivity and effectiveness, contributing to better user acceptance and confidence in the system. This incremental, or gradual, approach to innovation and change has its limitations. The tendency has been to modify and improve (at times dramatically) existing processes, but rarely to create new processes that replace existing processes. The result is sub-optimal, and we may incur a huge opportunity cost, as discussed later on.

The third problem identified above involves the dynamic nature of requirements. It was a breakthrough of sorts to explicitly recognize and accept that requirements will change over time, not only as a result of changes in the environment (e.g., the threat) but as a result of learning. Rather than treating this phenomenon as a flaw in the design and acquisition process, and tagging it with the inglorious label of requirements creep or growth, EA recognized it for what is was—the result of an interactive adaptive process.

When users expressed dissatisfaction with systems that met or exceeded their original specifications, it was a frustrating experience all around. In an effort to keep costs down, developers froze the specifications and ended any effective interaction between developers and users. The rationale was that the developers would not be distracted from their complex task of building the system. While this had the intended effect of reducing the costs associated with development and time to deliver systems, the price that was paid in operational effectiveness and user alienation was very high. EA recognized that this approach was counter-productive, and replaced it with the build-a-little, test-a-little, field-a-little strategy, with emphasis on a close-working relationship between users and operators.

As we begin to develop NCW applications, we would be well advised to keep in mind two key facts of life (recognized by EA), and leverage rather than fight them. The first, as identified above, is the need for users to become better acquainted with technology and its possibilities before they can intelligently develop NCW concepts. The second is to understand that these concepts must be allowed to evolve over time. To help ensure success, we should incorporate the following key components of EA into the process by which we coevolve MCPs:

1) continuous user involvement;
2) use of rapid prototypes to allow users to get tangible representations of the future;
3) build-a-little, test-a-little philosophy; and
4) develop an architecture that accommodates the changes that will surely come.

Role of Experimentation

Different kinds of experimentation will be needed at various points in the coevolution of NCW. There are three basic kinds of experimentation.[106] These include experiments designed to discover better ways of doing things, to test hypotheses, and to demonstrate (or confirm) what we believe as laws or facts. The first of these, Discovery Experiments, essentially generate hypotheses that are subsequently tested by Testing Experiments and confirmed by Demonstration Experiments. All experiments include, to one degree or another, assessments about the potential operational utility of an MCP, or part of an MCP.

Three classes of hypotheses need rigorous developing and testing on the road to NCW. The first involves the nature of shared awareness and what it takes to achieve it. The second involves the nature of self-synchronization and its mission-related utility. The third class of hypotheses that need to be tested involve the relationships between shared awareness and self-synchronization.

Role of Experimentation in the Coevolution of MCPs, Figure 35, presents an overview of the process by which concepts for new MCPs could be conceived, tested and retested, and finally transformed into a real operational capability. To achieve its goal, the MCP process focuses, synchronizes, and coordinates the efforts of numerous DoD organizations. Components of this MCP process currently exist, but the glue needed to hold these pieces together is weak, and the overall process itself is not as well

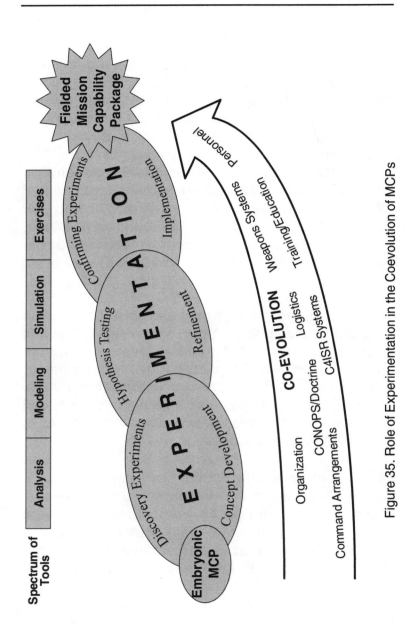

Figure 35. Role of Experimentation in the Coevolution of MCPs

focused as it could be. We currently are weakest in the front-end, or conceptual, phase and in accepting and implementing approaches that require changes in culture.

In the Concept Development Phase, groups of individuals, with the requisite operational and technical expertise, need to be brought together in a safe environment and with the charter to "think outside of the box." DoD needs to develop environments well suited to this task. Environments designed to facilitate innovation are expected to be an integral part of the process of Joint and Service Experimentation, and the designation of USJFCOM as the executive agent of Joint experimentation will help focus these efforts. While the need for experimentation is beginning to be widely accepted, there are different views on just what experimentation is all about. One size does not fit all as far as experimentation goes.

As concepts jell, they would be then subjected to a series of analyses, experiments, and tests to be refined to determine if they merit adoption by the DoD. It is essential to keep users heavily involved, insuring that each aspect of the package: command concepts and organization; doctrine and procedures; force packages; technology and systems; and training and education; is mutually supporting and operationally sound. The Concept Refinement Phase, having a distinctly hands-on flavor, is essential to facilitating effective communication among the communities.

DoD has invested in a full spectrum of models, simulations, testbeds, and instrumented ranges to support the testing of weapons, systems, equipment, doctrine, and concepts of operations for the training and exercising of our forces. While these valuable resources help to support the assessment and refinement of MCP concepts, several areas of weakness need to be addressed. Most urgently there is a need for explicit and flexible representation of command and control, and the effects associated with what has become known as information operations. While work needs to be done at all echelons of command, the most pressing need is at the CINC and JTF levels, with an emphasis on coalition operations. These models and simulations need to be able to accommodate changes in all aspects of the MCP, including doctrine, organizations, command approaches, lines of authority and information flows. Without this capability, these expensive investments will be unable to shed light on the critical issues being addressed by DoD. Equally obvious is that these models and tools no longer can be solely designed to support a particular segment of the community (e.g., training), but need to built with the idea that they will be used in all phases of the development of MCPs.

The last phase of the process requires the implementation of the institutional changes, technologies, and systems that are required by an MCP. At some point, a successful mission capability package concept will have gained sufficient credibility and the need for certain institutional changes will become widely recognized. This is a critical junction because it is here that the battle with the forces of inertia is joined. Given the knowledge of this battlefield in advance, it is important that the senior civilian and military leadership fully embrace the MCP process, and stay abreast of the development of MCP concepts and progress.

What is necessary is a mission-by-mission review of how we can meet the challenges we face. Since organizations need to continually accommodate change in the nature of their missions, the creation of structured "change processes" are required to facilitate and develop new MCP concepts and translate them into new operational capability.

Assessing the Potential of NCW

The DoD has a rich and diverse set of analytical tools and models that support analysis; unfortunately, few are suitable for the task of assessing the potential contributions of concepts, approaches, and systems based upon NCW. Many of our large detailed simulations were developed by and for the training community who were interested in developing and assessing competencies based upon current organizational structures and doctrine in the performance of tasks that contribute to traditional combat. These models are often hard wired for these purposes, and do not have the capability to reflect the very different set of assumptions, flow of information, or measures that are associated with NCW concepts of operations.

One reason that the analysis task is so challenging is the need to let more aspects of the problem vary. The application of NCW to a military situation or problem requires starting with a clean sheet of paper and designing a mission capability package from scratch, finding the most appropriate combination of a concept of operations, an approach to command and control, an organizational structure, a set of information flows, all to be matched with appropriate sensor and engagement capabilities. As we depart from the comfort of the status quo, we raise questions about expected performance that cannot be directly inferred from past experience. Warm and fuzzy feelings are unlikely to prove an acceptable substitute for solid analysis.

The key to any analysis (both its face validity and its utility) is the set of measures used to represent the performance and effectiveness of the alternatives being considered. We are relatively good at measuring the performance of sensors and actors, but less adept at measuring command and control. Command and control, to be fully understood, cannot be analyzed in isolation, but only in the context of the entire chain of events that close the sensor-to-actor loop. To make this even more challenging, we cannot isolate on one target or set of targets but need to consider the entire target set. Furthermore, NCW is not limited to attrition warfare, but is designed to support other concepts such as shock and awe. It is not sufficient to know how many targets were killed, but exactly which ones and when they were killed.

We have become better at characterizing the contribution of command and control as we have moved away from relying upon communications-focused measures like the probability of correct message receipt (PCMR) to targets at risk.[107] But we need to do more. Although using targets at risk is a great improvement in C4ISR analysis, it does not address a number of questions that are important for understanding NCW. The questions revolve around issues of battlespace awareness, planning, and execution. Targets at risk is a measure that combines aspects of each of these, but is essentially a measure of potential whose degree of realization is greatly dependent upon one or more aspects of an NCW-based approach to command and control, organizational, doctrine, training, and characteristics of the user interface (visualization). It is important for us to develop ways to characterize and reflect these attributes in our analyses and models.

Measures of Merit

One way to force the issue is to design a set of measures that focus our attention on these critical aspects of the problem. Some issues and questions that need to be explored to augment the targets at risk approach, and move it from a measure of potential to a measure of expectation, include:

1) Who in the battlespace is best equipped to make each firing decision?
2) Is the concept of operation, doctrine, organization, and training supportive of this?
3) How many decisions are expected to be needed, in what time frame, and to what extent is this feasible?
4) What is the impact of not allocating certain classes of decisions to specific individuals, but permitting overlaps (or gaps)?
5) Which decisions could be automated, and what is the best way to distribute the remaining decisions?
6) What information is most important to support time-critical decision making, and can it be made available to the individual responsible?

7) What is the impact of distributed teams sharing access to information and acting without prior synchronization?

The above questions illustrate the nature of the unknowns we need to explore if we are to make the most out of the opportunities afforded by the Information Age. To shed light on these issues, we will need empirical data and measures to guide our data collection and support analysis. This is why experimentation is critical to our efforts to transform NCW from a theory into practice.

At the heart of any assessment process are the measures of merit employed. In assessing the value of applying NCW to a variety of National Security missions and tasks, we will need to augment the measures we currently employ if we are to be able to better understand the impacts of NCW and the value of this new approach. It is one thing to adopt a new approach and compare the outcomes that result to a baseline case, and quite another to understand why different outcomes result. One might ask why this matters. What does our understanding buy us? After all, if we know that Approach B is better than Approach A, is this not enough? The answers to these questions lie in the complexity of applying NCW to military tasks. More information is not always better. More connectivity is not always better. More autonomy for actor entities is not always better. In many cases the response curve will increase for a while, then level off, and may at some point even go down. It is important to know the shape of these curves so we not only maximize mission-related measures, but also do so economically and efficiently. It will be important for us to know under what circumstances the MCP characteristics associated with NCW approach work and when they do not.

Currently, we think about five basic levels of measures (see Figure 36, Hierarchy of Measures). The first level involves measuring the performance of the C4ISR systems as federated into an infostructure, which is our computation power and ability to transmit or distribute information—connectivity and bandwidth. We have long recognized that increases in these measures do not *automatically* translate into increased mission success.

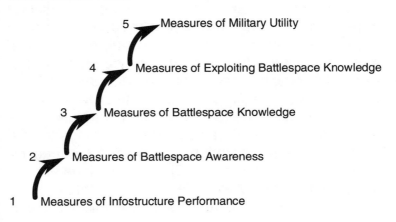

5 — Measures of Military Utility

4 — Measures of Exploiting Battlespace Knowledge

3 — Measures of Battlespace Knowledge

2 — Measures of Battlespace Awareness

1 — Measures of Infostructure Performance

Figure 36. Hierarchy of Measures

At the other end of the measurement hierarchy, we have measures related directly to mission effectiveness or utility. For combat operations, common measures that have been employed have included attrition rates, FEBA movement, fratricide, leakage, and time to accomplish a given mission. In our opinion, we must continue to work to improve these because neither do they often tell the whole story,[108] nor are they applicable to many of the missions we find ourselves undertaking in the Information Age. For example, the U.S. Navy in its analysis of the impact of IT-21 added *speed of command* to the traditional measures of time to objective, losses, high priority kills, and assets utilized.[109] OSD Net Assessment is undertaking a study to identify and explore the most promising measures of effectiveness for NCW.[110]

The fifth level (utility) was needed because some mission-related measures were found to be highly dependent upon scenario-related factors, and it was important to consider the robustness of a particular improvement. This fifth level involved a set of measures that portrayed the robustness of the alternative as a function of the scenario space. Recently, some have advocated explicit consideration of a sixth level, Measures of Policy Effectiveness. This level would allow us to assess the contribution of a military operation that was part of a larger undertaking, such as Peace Operations. There may indeed be cases where "successful" military operations are not sufficient to achieve policy objectives. In these cases it is important to understand the limits of military power.

Given this measurement hierarchy, we could address the question of whether an MCP was better than a baseline case, and we would be able to identify the impact it had on each of these five levels. But if we did not develop a set of measures that reflected NCW-related characteristics of the MCP, we would be unable to generalize or leverage the experiment. Put another way, in a particular case we might find that an MCP resulted in better information quality, better decision quality, and improved mission effectiveness, but it would not be proper to conclude that better information alone resulted in better decisions, or that better decisions alone resulted in improved mission effectiveness. An NCW-based MCP could be expected to differ in any number of ways from a non-NCW-based MCP. For example, organizational effects could be a key factor. We need to be able to identify and measure key features of NCW, measure them, and relate these characteristics to the measurement hierarchy.

The identification of key aspects of NCW-based MCPs needs to be addressed by the analytical community in close cooperation with the operational community. In tackling this task, we should bring to bear the fine work of many scientists from a number of different disciplines, ranging from cognitive scientists and organizational theorists, to those who study complexity.

How well the components of an MCP are matched will be of concern. For example, is the division of tasks matched to the dissemination of information? Are the decisions being made at the best time by the most qualified decision entity? Is the available battlespace knowledge being leveraged? We will want answers to these questions and others as we travel on our journey to implement NCW concepts. In other words, we want more out of our analyses than "B was better than A." We want to understand why, so we can apply the lessons learned to develop the best NCW-based MCPs.

The Journey Ahead

We are embarking upon a journey of discovery. The end state of our warfighting force in 2010 and beyond will emerge through a process of experimentation. There will be failures along the way. We will find that ideas that seemed promising could not be translated into combat power. Our success will depend upon our collective will, the preparations we make, and how we are provisioned. In this concluding chapter, the major challenges faced are identified, for it is only by being well prepared to meet these challenges that the journey will be a fruitful one.

The most significant challenges to be faced include:

1) the development of a shared understanding of the nature of national security in the Information Age;
2) the ability to work in a coalition environment;
3) the achievement of true jointness;
4) the coevolution of NCW-enabled MCPs;
5) the development and implementation of an investment strategy that supports NCW-enabled MCPs; and
6) the development of an appropriately skilled, educated, and trained force.

Security in the Information Age

The United States, as the only superpower, has yet to find a comfortable role in a changed world. However, it is clear that our role and the threats we face will be different and require us to adjust our view of missions, tools, and ourselves. Defending the nation and its vital interests in the future will involve more of an emphasis on asymmetrical threats and the conduct of operations other than war. Changes both in the geopolitical situation and advancing technology are driving the changes taking place in the security environment. Changes in the geopolitical environment have also resulted in the need to undertake significant operations in coalition environments. The proliferation of rapid advances in technology has put powerful weapons in the hands of a host of players, greatly increasing their significance and potential threat.

These weapons include both weapons of mass destruction (WMD) and the tools associated with information warfare, and in its most troubling form, infrastructure warfare. In some instances, the lines between peace and war and the distinctions among friend, foe, and neutral are becoming blurred beyond recognition.

Asymmetric warfare presents a unique set of challenges, not the least of which include finding successful strategies for deterrence, detection, and response. Lethal responses may become of little value in many situations when their political costs far outweigh their effects. Asymmetric warfare involves each side playing by its own set of rules, determined by their respective strengths and attempts to exploit an adversary's weakness. It is a far cry from the tank-on-tank battles or naval engagements of the past. This makes it very difficult to develop indications and warnings normally used to see if someone is preparing for war. Rather than working around the clock to produce airplanes or WMD, an adversary may be educating computer scientists.

If we look at these changes as a whole, it is clear that our missions have gotten to be far more complex, and our challenges and adversaries less predictable. The information that we need to sort things out has gotten, simultaneously, more diverse and more specific. Our measures of merit have also become more varied and complex, and our tool kit needs to be greatly expanded to properly address these more complex and varied situations. Dealing with this complexity will be a major challenge that requires approaching problems and tasks somewhat differently.

The term battlespace, instead of battlefield, has been used throughout this book to convey a sense of an expanded area and venue in which conflict occurs. The nature of the combatants in this battlespace is changing, and conflicts have become more public and less remote. Identifying combatants will be difficult because they will be spread out over a much wider area, either blending with their surroundings or not visible at all. Operations will be conducted in a fishbowl environment and information about events will be subject to public scrutiny in real time.

Understanding these new realities and developing appropriate strategies for dealing with them will be an ongoing challenge.

Coalition Environments

Whether in traditional military engagements, asymmetrical engagements, or in a variety of operations other than war, the United States will be working in coalition environments. Basic to the conduct of these operations is the ability to develop and maintain a shared perception of the situation, develop coherent plans that leverage the available resources, and execute them. This requires a level of information exchange, systems that can understand one another, a coalition-based planning process where all may participate, a common concept of operations, and a set of compatible procedures to carry out operations.

Given that future coalitions will be of the willing, and that they, at times, will contain former and future adversaries, achieving these prerequisites will be difficult indeed. Of greatest concern to some is that the United States, with its relatively enormous investments in technology, will become too sophisticated to interoperate with even its closest allies who cannot afford the price tags associated with the latest technologies. The need for a sufficient level of backward compatibility needs to be recognized, along with finding a way to achieve this without degrading our own performance. This is a major challenge, both technically and operationally.

Jointness

Jointness is a relatively recent concept and is now gaining momentum. In order to satisfy the needs of NCW, jointness needs to be more than skin-deep. It needs to be built-in from the bottom up, so that the best way to accomplish a mission or task, given the available information and assets, can be employed. There are significant institutional barriers to achieve *born joint* MCPs. To maximize our chances of success, we need to foster true jointness in the process of coevolution, investment strategy, and education and training efforts.

Process of Coevolution

The process of coevolution needs to differ from previous processes that served to introduce change and technology into organizations in a number of ways. First, the introduction of technology in the form of a system, or set of materials, is no longer the focus or objective. Rather, the objective is a set of NCW-based MCPs. Hence the degree of the changes required is much greater, as is the number of organizations that need to be involved. Second, adequate emphasis needs to be placed on MCPs being born joint, otherwise it is likely that stove-piped MCPs will be produced. Chances are these stove-piped MCPs will represent incremental improvements, but fail to take full advantage of the opportunities. Third, coevolution is a process of discovery and testing. The answer will not be known in advance. Thus, the process needs to be devoid of the pass/fail mentality common today. Fourth, the heart of the coevolution process is experimentation, not demonstrations nor exercises, although there is a role, albeit a reduced one, for both of these in the process. Fifth, the process is iterative. One cannot expect to get it right the first time out. However, one can expect that events will be planned and conducted to get the most knowledge out of the experience as possible.

Investment Strategy

Individual services and agencies currently acquire material and systems one by one. This approach needs to change. Instead, DoD needs to develop investment strategies and make acquisition decisions based upon portfolios. Two kinds of portfolios need to be considered. The first is a portfolio or package of investments that mirrors an MCP. The second is an infrastructure portfolio consisting of a set of capabilities necessary to support multiple MCPs in a specific area such as communications. The trade-offs that need to be made include:

1) the overall mix of MCPs to be deployed;
2) which alternate MCP configurations should be adopted for a particular mission; and
3) the components of a federation of supporting systems (including combat support, personnel, finance, etc.).

It also needs to be recognized that accounting procedures must not get in the way of making intelligent choices. Currently, expense items are not visible in the same way that capital investments are, despite the fact that the items acquired need to be part of the same portfolio. Given a budget that is unlikely to increase in real dollars and a continuing, if not increasing, tension between modernization and readiness, the systemic suboptimality inherent in current practices needs to be addressed.

Education and Training

Change is difficult. Big changes are more difficult. The adoption of NCW will involve significant, if not fundamental changes in how DoD task organizes duties and responsibilities of individuals. Individuals will need to adopt new attitudes, accept more responsibility, learn new skills, master new approaches, and operate new systems—all in a faster-paced environment. The future DoD is likely to have fewer, but more educated and highly trained individuals. Current up-and-out and job-rotation personnel practices will need to be reexamined in the face of these changes. A hard look at our whole approach to education and training is required. Given the pace of change, education and training will need to be continuous and closely integrated with day-to-day activities. Distance learning and on-the-job training, employing sophisticated tools embedded in operational systems, will become the norm. A major consideration is that we are moving away from a situation in which we knew how we wanted a particular task performed, and then designed tools and processes to teach known solutions. We are now entering a period where we will not know the answer at the start of the process, and the techniques and tools that are associated with education and training may no longer be valid.[111]

It is fitting that this book on NCW concludes with this discussion of the impact on people. The C4ISR

Cooperative Research Program has been involved in a number of lessons learned analyses of deployments and operations. An observation common to all of these was the critical contribution that individuals had upon the success of these operations. Individuals were able to overcome unfavorable initial conditions, adapt outmoded approaches and processes, and provide the work necessary to integrate technology that simply was not yet ready for prime time. If NCW is to be successful, every effort must be made to recruit, educate, and train the right people, and give them the flexibility to make the necessary adjustments.

Bringing It All Together

The Information Revolution is upon us. It is not about information technology per se. Rather it is about how information-enabled organizations are emerging as dominant forces in their respective domains. Even at this early stage in the Information Revolution we have seen how organizational forms, processes, and applications of technology have coevolved. In the commercial sector, market forces provide a continuous forcing function for coevolution. In the domain of warfare, the forcing function is discontinuous. In previous generations, warfighting concepts and capabilities have evolved slowly, if not at all during interwar periods. This is not to say that innovative ideas were not born and nurtured, during interwar periods, but rather, that with rare exceptions, they were not brought to full fruition and implemented. The crucible of war creates a new competitive dynamic. New ideas and concepts have a better opportunity to see the light of day because it often becomes clear that current operational concepts are failing.[112] Changes are accelerated and compressed into the time frame of war. Most anticipate that future conflicts will be much shorter in duration, thus not providing as good an opportunity for coevolution. Thus, without reversing this trend, we will not be able to fully realize the opportunities provided by information technologies to transform the way we do business. Our commitment to experimentation at the Joint and Service level can provide the necessary but not sufficient forcing function for the coevolution of a network-centric force. Exploiting the insights we develop through experimentation requires more. Leadership will be necessary to ensure that:

1) conditions for innovation exist at all levels;
2) promising new ideas have a chance to develop and reach maturity; and
3) legacy ideas and their manifestations do not crowd out their "competition."

This is an exciting time.

Endnotes

1 VAdm Arthur K. Cebrowski, USN, and John J. Garstka, "Network Centric Warfare: Its Origin and Future," *Proceedings of the Naval Institute* 124:1 (January 1998): 28–35.

2 Adm Jay L. Johnson, Chief of Naval Operations (CNO), USN, in his address at the U.S. Naval Institute Annapolis Seminar and 123rd Annual Meeting, in Annapolis, Maryland, on April 23, 1997, said the military is in the midst of "a fundamental shift from what we call platform-centric warfare to something we call network-centric warfare."

3 U.S. Air Force, *The Army Air Forces in World War II—Vol. I: Plans and Operations, January 1939–August 1942* (Chicago: University of Chicago Press, 1948), 597–611.

4 U.S. Air Force, *The Army Air Forces in World War II—Vol. III: Europe: Argument to VE Day, January 1944–May 1945* (Washington, DC: Office of Air Force History, 1983), 49.

5 Richard Hough and Denis Richards, *The Battle of Britain* (New York: W. W. Norton and Company, 1989).

6 Stephen C. Mooney, *The Cyberstate* (Denver, CO: ACM, Inc., 1996).

7 Robert G. Phelan, Jr. and Michael L. McGinnis, "Reengineering the United States Army's Tactical Command and Control Operational Architecture for Information Operations," *Proceedings of the 1996 Winter Simulation Conference*, 1996.

8 Richard Saul Wurman, *Information Anxiety* (New York: Bantam Books, 1990).

9 *Ibid.*

[10] M. Mitchell Waldrop, *Complexity: The Emerging Science at the Edge of Chaos* (New York: Simon and Schuster, 1992), 259–260.

[11] Peter Newcomb, "The First Billion Takes a Lifetime…Except in the Internet Age," *Forbes* 163:8 (April 19, 1999): 246–247.

[12] T. X. Hammes, "War Isn't a Rational Business," *Proceedings of the Naval Institute* 124:7 (July 1998): 22–25.

[13] U.S. Department of Commerce, "IT Industries—Of Growing Importance to the Economy and Jobs," Appendix 1 in *The Emerging Digital Economy* (Washington, DC: Government Printing Office).

[14] Michael E. Porter, *Competitive Advantage: Creating and Sustaining Superior Performance* (New York: Free Press, 1985).

[15] Charles B. Stabel, et al., "Configuring Value for Competitive Advantage: On Chains, Shops, and Networks," *Strategic Management Journal* 19 (1998), 413–437.

[16] "George Gilder's Telecosm: Metcalfe's Law and Legacy," *Forbes ASAP* 152: Supplement (September 1993), 158–166. Metcalfe's Law is named after Robert Metcalfe, who invented the staple networking topology, Ethernet. Metcalfe's Law of the telecosm states that the potential value of a network is "n" squared, with "n" being the number of nodes on the network.

[17] *CIO Imperative: Business Results Are the End—Information Sharing Is the Means*, The Concours Group, 1997.

[18] Don Tapscott, *The Digital Economy: Promise and Peril in the Age of Networked Intelligence* (New York: McGraw–Hill, 1996), 143–152.

[19] Karl Sabbagh, *Twenty-First Century Jet: The Making and Marketing of the Boeing 777* (New York: Scribner, 1996).

[20] Carl W. Stern, "The Deconstruction of Value Chains," *Perspectives*, The Boston Consulting Group, September 1998.

[21] Karl Sabbagh, *Twenty-First Century Jet: The Making and Marketing of the Boeing 777* (New York: Scribner, 1996).

[22] *Capitalizing on Innovation*, Capital One's 1998 Debt Equity Conference, October 20, 1998.

[23] www.dell.com

[24] Joan Magretta, "The Power of Virtual Integration: An Interview with Dell Computer's Michael Dell," *Harvard Business Review* 76:2 (March–April 1998), 72–84.

[25] www.compaq.com

[26] Don Tapscott, *The Digital Economy: Promise and Peril in the Age of Networked Intelligence* (New York: McGraw–Hill, 1996), 84, 101, 131.

[27] *Ibid.*

[28] "The Leaders in 1997 Sales and Profits," *Business Week* 3567 (March 2, 1998), 110.

[29] James F. Moore*, The Death of Competition: Leadership and Strategy in the Age of Business Ecosystems* (New York: HarperBusiness, 1996), 161–188.

[30] Christopher Palmeri, "Believe in Yourself, Believe in the Merchandise," *Forbes* 160:5 (September 8, 1997), 118–124.

[31] Frank Swoboda, "Talking Management with Chairman Welch," *The Washington Post* (March 23, 1997, Section H: Business), 1, 7.

[32] John Foley, "Squeezing More Value from Data," *Information Week* (December 9, 1996), 44.

33 Matthew Schifrin and Erika Brown, "Merrill's Malaise," *Forbes* 163:7 (April 5, 1999), 108–114.

34 Merrill Lynch Site Visits, August 11, 1997 and October 28, 1997.

35 Seth Schiesel, "The No. 1 Customer: Sorry It Isn't You," *The New York Times* (November 23, 1997, Section 3: Money & Business), 1, 10.

36 Interviews with Christopher J. Carroll, Managing Director, Head of Global Electronic Trading, Deutsche Morgan Grenfell, Inc., 1996–1997.

37 VAdm Arthur K. Cebrowski, USN, "Network Centric Warfare: An Emerging Military Response to the Information Age," Presentation to the 1999 Command and Control Research and Technology Symposium, Naval War College, Newport, RI, June 29, 1999.

38 David S. Alberts and Richard E. Hayes, *Command Arrangements for Peace Operations* (Washington, DC: National Defense University Press, 1995); David S. Alberts, *Operations Other Than War: The Technological Dimension* (Washington, DC: National Defense University Press, 1995); Margaret Daly Hayes and Gary F. Wheatley, *Interagency and Political-Military Dimensions of Peace Operations: Haiti—A Case Study* (Washington, DC: National Defense University Press, 1996); Tom Czerwinski, *Coping with the Bounds: Speculations on Nonlinearity in Military Affairs* (Washington, DC: National Defense University Press, 1998); Larry Wentz, *Lessons from Bosnia: The IFOR Experience* (Washington, DC: National Defense University Press, 1998); Martin C. Libicki, *What Is Information Warfare?* (Washington, DC, National Defense University Press, 1995); and Martha Maurer, *Coalition Command and Control: Key Considerations* (Washington, DC: National Defense University Press, 1994).

39 David S. Alberts, *Command and Control in Peace Operations*, [report on "Western Hemisphere Experience in

Global Peace Operations," the third of a series of reports of workshops organized by the INSS Center for Advanced Command Concepts and Technology (ACTS)] (Washington, DC: National Defense University Press, 1995).

[40] *Ibid.*

[41] Martin C. Libicki, *What Is Information Warfare?* (Washington, DC: National Defense University Press, 1995).

[42] Stuart E. Johnson and Martin C. Libicki, "DBK and Its Consequences," in *Dominant Battlespace Knowledge* (Washington, DC: National Defense University Press, 1995), 34.

[43] Kenneth Allard, *Somalia Operations: Lessons Learned* (Washington, DC: National Defense University Press, 1995).

[44] Joseph A. Welch, Jr., "State of the Art of C2 Assessment," *Proceedings for Quantitative Assessment of the Utility of Command and Control System*, MTR 80W00025 (January 1980), 11.

[45] For details on Lawson's model, see "Naval Tactical C3 Architecture, 1985–1995," *Signal* 33:10 (August 1979), 71–72.

[46] For details, contact Evidence Based Research, Inc., at www.ebrinc.com

[47] Kenneth Allard, *Command, Control, and the Common Defense*, revised edition (Washington, DC: National Defense University Press, 1996).

[48] Interviews with RAdm Charles R. McGrail, USN (Ret.), 1996-1998.

[49] Larry Wentz, *Lessons from Bosnia: The IFOR Experience* (Washington, DC: National Defense University Press, 1998).

[50] Pascale Combelles Siegel, *Target Bosnia: Integrating Information Activities in Peace Operations* (Washington, DC: National Defense University Press, 1998).

[51] Manuel de Landa, *War in the Age of Intelligent Machines* (New York: Zone Books, 1991); John T. Dockerty and A. E. R. Woodcock, *The Military Landscape: Mathematical Models of Combat* (Cambridge, UK: Woodhead, 1993); Murray Gell-Mann, *The Quark and the Jaguar* (New York, W.H. Freeman, 1994); John Gore, *Chaos, Complexity, and the Military* (Washington, DC: National Defense University, 1996); Glenn E. James, *Chaos Theory: The Essentials for Military Applications* Newport Paper 10 (Newport, RI: Naval War College, 1996); and Edward N. Lorenz, *The Essence of Chaos* (Seattle, WA: University of Washington Press, 1993). For more, see David S. Alberts and Thomas J. Czerwinski, "Working Bibliography," *Complexity, Global Politics, and National Security* (Washington, DC: National Defense University Press, 1997), 333–381.

[52] David S. Alberts, *Lessons Learned from ISX 1.1*, AIAA Joint Experiment Task Force Briefing, January 28, 1999.

[53] *Knowledge and Speed: The Annual Report on the Army After Next Project to the Chief of Staff of the Army*, July 1997.

[54] *Executive Summary of Global '98 Wargame*, Naval War College, Newport, RI, July 13–31, 1998.

[55] *Ibid.*

[56] *Ibid.*

[57] *Ibid.*

[58] David A. Fulghum, "Improved Air Defenses Prompt Pentagon Fears," *Aviation Week & Space Technology* 149:1 (July 6, 1998), 22–24.

[59] VAdm Arthur K. Cebrowski, USN, and John J. Garstka, "Network Centric Warfare: Its Origin and Future," *Proceedings of the Naval Institute* 124:1 (January, 1998), 28–35.

[60] Adm Jay L. Johnson, CNO, USN, Address at the U.S. Naval Institute Annapolis Seminar and 123rd Annual Meeting, Annapolis, MD, April 23, 1997.

[61] David S. Alberts, *The Unintended Consequences of Information Age Technologies* (Washington, DC: National Defense University Press, 1996), 35–36.

[62] *Executive Summary of Global '98 Wargame*, Naval War College, Newport, RI, July 13–31, 1998.

[63] *Ibid.*

[64] Gen. Charles A. Horner, USAF (Ret.), "Comments on Expeditionary Force Experiment '98," *C2 Earlybird: Special Edition EFX '98 Lessons Learned* 1: Special Ed.1 (December 1998).

[65] Robert M. Nutwell, "IT-21 Provides Big 'Reachbacks'," *Proceedings of the Naval Institute* 124:1 (January 1998), 36–38.

[66] Adm Jay L. Johnson, CNO, USN, CNO Address at AFCEA West, San Diego, CA, January 21, 1998.

[67] R. Thomas Goodden, et al., *Education Technology in Support of Joint Professional Military Education in 2010: The EdTech Report* (Washington, DC: A Joint Staff Publication, October 1998).

[68] *Tactics, Techniques, and Procedures for the Common Operational Modeling, Planning, and Simulation Strategy (COMPASS), Version 1.1*, JWID Joint Project Office, August 31, 1998.

[69] In addition to sensor, decision maker, and actor entities that work together to achieve and utilize battlespace awareness, there are supporting entities that structure the flow of material and systems that process battlespace information.

[70] A common operational picture does not imply that everyone in the battlespace sees exactly the same thing, in the same way, at the same time. Rather it means that at least a subset of the people have the same information available about key components of battlespace awareness in a timely manner. The effect is that they share a common perception of the situation. This common perception enables better communication and mutually supporting actions.

[71] Sarah Cliffe, "Knowledge Management: The Well-Connected Business," *Harvard Business Review* 76:4 (July–August 1998), 17–21.

[72] Air Force Space Command/Space Warfare Center, *Information Briefing on Capabilities of Space Warfare Center/Shield Program*, Colorado Springs, CO, 1998.

[73] *Sensor-to-Shooter C4 Battle Management, Final Report* (Washington, DC: C4ISR Decision Support Center and Joint Chiefs of Staff Directorate for C4 Systems, April 1, 1999).

[74] William K. Stevens, "Naval Simulation System: Representation of Network Centric Warfare Concepts and Architectures," *Proceedings of the SMi Conference on Network Centric Warfare*, June 23-24, 1999, London.

[75] Andy McNab, *Bravo Two Zero*, New York, Island Books, 1994, 25-28.

[76] See U.S. Marine Corps, *Beyond C2: A Concept for Comprehensive Command and Coordination of the Marine Air-Ground Task Force* (Washington, DC: Headquarters, U.S. Marine Corps, June 1998).

⁷⁷ David S. Alberts and Thomas J. Czerwinski, "Working Bibliography," *Complexity, Global Politics, and National* Security (Washington, DC: National Defense University Press, 1997), 333–381; and Tom Czerwinski, *Coping with the Bounds: Speculations on Nonlinearity in Military Affairs* (Washington, DC: National Defense University Press, 1998). Also, visit the Santa Fe Institute Internet homepage at www.santafe.edu

⁷⁸ The word "system" here should not be taken to mean computer systems, but refers to a collection of interacting individuals and organizations, along with their processes and tools.

⁷⁹ VAdm Arthur K. Cebrowski, USN, and John J. Garstka, "Network Centric Warfare: Its Origin and Future," *Proceedings of the Naval Institute* 124:1 (January 1998), 28–35.

⁸⁰ *Knowledge and Speed: The Annual Report on the Army After Next Project to the Chief of Staff of the Army*, July 1997.

⁸¹ John A. Tirpak, "Deliberate Force," *Air Force* 80:10 (October 1987).

⁸² Tempo here refers to the pace of the engagement, how fast decisions are made and acted upon, and how many simultaneous decision/action threads can be concurrent. Operating tempo is a different term that has been used to describe the utilization of equipment. A high operating tempo means that the useful life (in calendar time) of a piece of equipment will reduce and/or increase maintenance costs.

⁸³ Maneuver also includes being put in the right place the first time.

⁸⁴ "The Cooperative Engagement Capability," *Johns Hopkins APL Technical Digest* 16:4 (1995), 377–396.

⁸⁵ *Sensor to Shooter III: Precision Engagement C4ISR Architecture Analysis, Final Report* (Washington, DC: C4ISR

Decision Support Center and Joint Chiefs of Staff Directorate for C4 Systems, June 15, 1997).

[86] VAdm Arthur K. Cebrowski, USN, and John J. Garstka, "Network Centric Warfare: Its Origin and Future," *Proceedings of the Naval Institute* 124:1 (January 1998), 28–35.

[87] Interview of MG William S. Wallace, CG 4th ID, USA, Fort Hood, TX, January 20, 1999.

[88] VAdm Arthur K. Cebrowski, USN, Written testimony to hearing on Defense Information Superiority and Information Assurance— Entering the 21st Century, held by House Armed Services Committee, subcommittee on military research and development and subcommittee on military procurement, February 23, 1999.

[89] BG William L. Bond, USA, *Army Digitization Overview*, Briefing to Dr. Jacques Gansler, USD (A&T), at the Pentagon, Arlington, VA, on May 20, 1998.

[90] BG William L. Bond, USA, *Military CIS '98*, Briefing to Dr. Jacques Gansler, USD (A&T), at the Pentagon, Arlington, VA, on April 20, 1998.

[91] http://efx.acc.af.mil, updated 01/21/99.

[92] *Smart Card in Cobra Gold '98: Business Case Analysis— Final Report*, Department of Defense Smart Card Technology Office, January 1999. [Report available at www.dmdc.osd.mil/smartcard].

[93] Harlan Ullman, James Wade, Jr. et al., *Shock and Awe: Achieving Rapid Dominance* (Washington, DC: National Defense University Press, 1996).

[94] Artificial because the limits are the result of how we choose to distribute responsibility and utilize information rather than the results of information availability and quality.

[95] Sherry Sontag and Christopher Drew, *Blind Man's Bluff: The Untold Story of American Submarine Espionage*, Public Affairs™, 1998.

[96] LTG Douglas D. Buchholz, USA, Written testimony to hearing on defense transformation, held by Senate Armed Services Committee, subcommittee on airland forces, March 4, 1998.

[97] VAdm Arthur K. Cebrowski, USN, and John J. Garstka, "Network Centric Warfare: Its Origin and Future," *Proceedings of the Naval Institute* 124:1 (January 1998), 28–35.

[98] Michael S. Frankel and Robert H. Gormley, "Achieving Information Dominance: The Integrated Information Infrastructure—A Vision for the 21st Century," *SRI International Study Report*, September 17, 1998.

[99] *CISCO Internetwork Operating System—Release 12.0*, CISCO Systems, Copyright 1989–1998.

[100] Website for Report of President's Commission on Critical Infrastructure Protection, [www.rstcorp.com/ieee/archives], March 1999.

[101] Lt.Gen. John L. Woodward, USAF, Written testimony to hearing on Defense Information Superiority and Information Assurance—Entering the 21st Century, held by House Armed Services Committee, subcommittee on military research and development and subcommittee on military procurement, February 23, 1999.

[102] That is, they no longer result from a directed search for an improved capability to fill a perceived existing or projected operational shortfall (e.g., more accurate, longer range weapons, stealth technology, improved armor).

[103] AFCEA Study Team, *Evolutionary Acquisition Study* (Fairfax, VA: AFCEA, June 7, 1993).

[104] *Ibid.*

[105] David S. Alberts, *Lessons Learned from ISX 1.1*, AIAA Joint Experiment Task Force Briefing, January 28, 1999.

[106] These ideas were developed by an AIAA Task Force on C2 Experimentation.

[107] *Sensor to Shooter III: Precision Engagement C4ISR Architecture Analysis, Final Report* (Washington, DC: C4ISR Decision Support Center and Joint Chiefs of Staff Directorate for C4 Systems, June 15, 1997).

[108] Joseph A. Welch, Jr., "State of the Art of C2 Assessment," *Proceedings for Quantitative Assessment of the Utility of Command and Control System*, MTR 80W00025 (January 1980), 11.

[109] Adm Archie R. Clemins, USN, "Naval Simulation System (NSS): An Assessment of IT-21 Warfighting Value-Added," Briefing, January 5, 1999.

[110] *Measuring the Effects of Network-Centric Warfare* (Draft, Unpublished), Office of the Secretary of Defense (Net Assessment), Pentagon, Arlington, VA.

[111] Obviously, at any given point in time, we need to settle in on the tasks to be accomplished, associated doctrine, and a set of systems. However, a significant amount of effort needs to be devoted to developing new approaches and systems if we are to adopt NCW and that we will, in future, evolve these far more rapidly than we evolve current practices and systems. Therefore, our approach to education and training needs to be adapted to the task of developing NCW MCPs and evolving them.

[112] U.S. Air Force, *The Army Air Forces in World War II—Vol I: Plans and Operations, January 1939–August 1942* (Chicago: University of Chicago Press, 1948), 666–668.

Appendix A
Information Technology Trends and the Value-Creation Potential of Networks

Information technology and the "networks" they enable play a fundamental role in enabling the network-centric enterprise. Consequently, understanding the underlying trends that govern technology and influence the value-creation potential of networks is important to understanding the potential power of network-centric operations.

The basic building block of a network-centric enterprise is the entity. Entities work both individually and collectively to create the value generated by network-centric operations. The nature of their interactions is enabled or constrained by the characteristics of the technology that is available to these entities and which governs the interactions among them. For example, if entities can only interact via mail, then the nature of their information exchanges will differ significantly from entities that can instantly interact in a multi-media environment (e.g., video teleconferencing).

Technologies that are associated with linking entities include: telephones, radios, fax machines, televisions, computers, and personal digital assistants. Networking systems provide the functional capability to direct information from one node to another. In most large networks, large numbers of networking devices are employed to direct information among nodes. Links provide transmission paths among networking devices and nodes, as well as gateways to other networks.

With modern voice networks, nodes consist of telephones. Optimized networking systems provide quality of service for voice traffic (e.g., PBX switches). Transmission mediums include wire line, fiber, and radio frequency.

With cable networks, nodes consist of cable boxes connected to customers' televisions and signal broadcasting centers providing signals that are distributed over the cable network. Until recently, cable networks were designed principally to operate in half-duplex mode; that is, signals travel in only one direction—from the broadcast node to the set-top box.

With modern data networks, nodes are digital and networking systems (e.g., routers, Asynchronous Transfer Mode (ATM) switches) are optimized for data traffic. As with voice networks, transmission lines include wire line, fiber, or radio frequency.

Military operations employ commercial information technologies, as well as military specific information technologies. In general, the primary difference between the networks used by deployed warfighters and the networks used by non-mobile entities is the characteristics of the links. The primary transmission path for the deployed warfighter is radio frequency communications enabled by radio, data link, or satellite. Furthermore, military operations typically require special link features, such as security and anti-jam, which to date have not been priorities for commercial users.

There are a number of fundamental business and technology trends that are shaping the future of networks, the nature of the nodes that are connected to networks, and the future of network-centric operations.

Moore's Law—2x Every 18 Months

Moore's Law describes the principle dynamic of innovation in the semiconductor fabrication market. In 1965, Gordon E. Moore, then R&D Director at Fairchild Semiconductor and presently Chairman Emeritus of Intel Corporation, observed that semiconductor manufacturers had been doubling the density of components per integrated circuit at regular intervals from 1959 to 1964. Furthermore, he asserted (based on three data points!) that this trend was poised to continue for the foreseeable future (at least the next 10 years). Upon reexamination by Moore in 1975, the regular interval turned out to be approximately 18 months. The net result is that for the past 45 years the performance of computer chips has doubled approximately every 18 months as a direct result of increasing component density. It is worth noting that the performance of dynamic Random Access Memory (dRAM) chips has increased at a faster rate than computer chips. Multiple factors have interacted to enable this remarkable run, which to a large degree is the direct result of the innovation and leadership of a wide range of companies. These companies range from the chip producers themselves (i.e., Intel, AMD, Motorola, Texas Instruments), to the companies that design and produce the semiconductor fabrication equipment used by the chip producers (i.e., Applied Materials, Lam Research, Novellus Systems).[1]

The limits to continued progress in increasing the density of semiconductor processing chips based on silicon technology are defined by physics. Scientists at Bell Laboratories recently identified that fundamental limits to chip density will be approached in 2012, when semiconductor gate sizes reach atomic limits.[2]

The same technology trends which have enabled the performance-cost ratio for personal computers to double approximately every 18 months have also enabled relatively small, powerful chips to be deployed in a wide variety of devices, such as personal digital assistants (PDAs). The net result is that the metric for measuring the degree of adoption of computer technology has been redefined several times from the percentage of households that own a computer to the number of computers per household to the number of computing devices per individual. In addition a new metric, percent of households connected to the Internet, has come into use. Analogous trends are being played out in warfare as we make the shift to network-centric operations.

---

[1] Michael Murphy, *Every Investors Guide to High-Tech Stocks and Mutual Funds* (New York, Broadway Books, 1997), 49-74.

[2] David A. Muller, et al, "The Electronic Structure at the Atomic Scale of Ultrathin Gate Oxides," *Nature*, Volume 399, June 24, 1999, 758-761.

Transmission Capacity—2x Every 12 Months

Currently, the primary backbone of advanced networks (both voice and data) is fiber optic cable. Recent and ongoing developments in the field of optical communications have resulted in the doubling of the transmission capacity of fiber optic cable every 12 months. The core technology behind this increased performance is dense wave division multiplexing that enables multiple wavelengths of light to be transmitted simultaneously over a single cable. Four key enabling technologies are at the core of the performance increases in dense wave division multiplexing:

1) sources of multiple wavelengths;
2) tunable optical filters;
3) wavelength multiplexers/demultiplexers; and
4) multiwavelength optical amplifiers.[3]

This performance trend in fiber optical communications is key to enabling the significant capacity increase of the Internet. It is also the source of the assertion made by many that in the near future, terrestrial bandwidth will be a commodity.[4] In addition, companies such as Teledesic are pursuing efforts to launch large constellations of satellites to provide high capacity bandwidth worldwide over radio frequency.

---

[3] Alan E. Willner, "Mining the Optical Bandwidth for a Tera Bit Per Second," *IEEE Spectrum,* April 1997, 32-41.

[4] Seth Schiesel, "Jumping Off the Bandwidth Wagon: Long Distance Carriers Regroup," *The New York Times* (July 3, 1999, Section 3: Money & Business), 1, 10, 11.

Confluence of Trends—Network-Centric Computing

The consequences of these mutually reinforcing trends have been profound. The combination of increasing performance and cost suppression has resulted in the widespread adoption of computers in business and in the home which, when combined with trends in communications, has set the stage for network-centric computing and network-centric operations. The combination of digital communications capabilities and breakthroughs in software technology in the form of Web browsers and servers has combined to enable information interactions among entities of virtually any size that can be connected to the Internet. The net result is referred to by some as the social-technological phenomenon, the "Internet Tsunami."

Metcalfe's Law

Metcalfe's Law, named after Robert Metcalfe, inventor of the ethernet protocol technology and founder of 3Com, has emerged as a central metaphor for the Internet Age.[5] Metcalfe's Law observes that although the cost of deploying a network increases linearly with the number of nodes in the network, the *potential* value of a network increases (scales) as a function of the square of the number of nodes that are connected by the network.

Business Trends—Convergence of Voice and Data

The confluence of these technology trends is creating new business opportunities and outmoding existing business models in the communications and

---

[5] George Gilder's Telecosm, "Metcalfe's Law and Legacy," *Forbes ASAP*, September 13, 1993, 158-166.

computing sectors. In the computing sector, the dramatic increase in computer performance enabled by Moore's Law has resulted in the introduction of entry-level systems at the $500-price point. As a result of this trend, profit margins for entry-level personal computers have been significantly reduced. Associated with this trend is an emerging business strategy that calls for personal computers to be given away virtually for free as loss leaders by Internet Service Providers. A consequence of these developments is the emergence of data traffic (vice voice) as the primary method of information transmission. Data traffic over the Internet is currently doubling every 7.5 months, while voice traffic over the Internet core is doubling every 4 months.[6] Consequently, the transmission of data is primary organizing logic for 21st-century networks. Networks are currently being, and will continue to be, optimized to simultaneously handle voice, data, and video over digital networks.

Implications of Metcalfe's Law

The discussion that follows explores the underlying logic behind Metcalfe's Law, the meaning of "value," and the need for extending the law with corollaries that account for networks with different performance attributes.

Much of the confusion over the meaning of Metcalfe's Law has to do with the definition of "value." The number of *potential* first order information interactions enabled by a network with N entities is computed as Nx(N-1).

---

[6] Rich Roca, "AT&T Bell Labs Presentation on Information Technology Trends to GovTechNet '99," Washington, DC, June 16, 1999.

Consequently, as will be clear from the derivation that follows, Metcalfe's Law asserts that if the metric for measuring value is the number of potential information interactions enabled, then for large N this value increases exponentially as N^2.

However, this approach to measuring value has its problems. It assumes that:

1) there is real potential in all interactions;
2) all interactions have positive value;
3) all interactions have equal value; and
4) the sum of a pair of wise interactions reflect the overall value.

In addition, it does not account for the nature of the simultaneous interactions among multiple entities.

We believe that the *potential* for a network to *create value* is a function of the type of the information interactions enabled by the network and the value-creation logic being employed by the users of the network. Thus, e*stablishing a direct relationship between information and value is at the heart of value creation in the Information Age and is fundamental to understanding the power of network-centric operations.* In addition, we believe that:

1) most potential interactions will never take place;
2) the value of interactions will differ significantly;
3) there will be islands of dense and intense interactions that will dominate the value function;

4) the value of a given interaction will be a function of the content, quality, and timeliness of the interaction; and
5) N-way interactions will be the most significant in value creation.

The following examples provide useful insights into the derivation of the value scaling properties of networks, as well as the need for associating with a network the concept of value-creation logic and user-value preferences (sometimes referred to as a utility function).

The largest networks (in terms of number of entities) that exist today are telecommunications networks. These networks represent hundreds of billions of dollars in investments made over a period of decades by telephone companies. The existence of these networks paved the way for the Internet because it provided the initial backbone of the Internet, as well as the "last mile" that connected the majority of customers to Internet service providers.

Telephone networks had been deployed widely when the fax machine, representing a new type of interaction, was first introduced.[7] When the first fax machines were installed they had limited value because there were very few other fax machines to connect to and to exchange information with.

As the size of the installed base of fax machines increased, the potential number of information

---

[7] Valerie-Anne Giscard d'Estang and Mark Young, *Inventions and Discoveries 1993,* New York, Facts on File, 1993, 198.

interactions among fax machines increased exponentially. The following very simple example of a network of entities that interact via fax demonstrates how the number of potential information interactions in a network is computed.

One fax machine has zero value to a user because it cannot transmit or send information to any other fax machines. As soon as a second fax machine is added, two information interactions are enabled. Fax 1 can fax to Fax 2, and Fax 2 can fax to Fax 1. These interactions are portrayed in Figure A-1(a). Once Fax 3 is added, we observe that the number of potential information interactions increases significantly, as portrayed in Figure A-1(b). The total number of interactions is six.

We observe that in general, if a network contains "N" entities, every entity can initiate "N-1" information interactions. Therefore the total number of potential value-creating interactions is: $N \times (N-1)$ or $N^2 - N$. For large values of N, the potential number of value-creating interactions in a network scales with N^2 or "N squared." Thus, Metcalfe's Law asserts that to the first order, the potential value of a network is a function of the number of potential information interactions between networked entities.

However, this is a gross oversimplification because, as we observe above, not all interactions are of equal value. We need to quantify user value as a function of the type of information interactions that are enabled (the content, quality, and timeliness of information exchanged), network-enabled, value-creation logic, and user-value preferences.

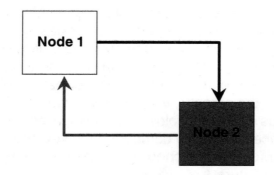

(a) Network with 2 Nodes (N=2)
Number of Information Interactions=2x1=2

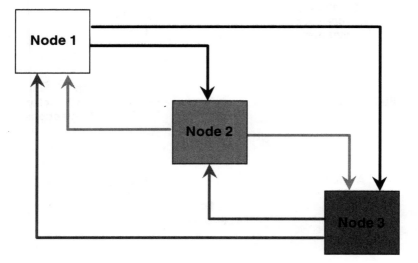

(b) Network with 3 Nodes (N=3)
Number of Information Interactions=3x2=6

Figure A-1. Entity Interactions

For example, if we applied the scaling logic of Metcalfe's Law to a network of e-mail-enabled entities, it would yield the same results as when applied to a network of fax-enabled entities. Clearly that would be incorrect, for the potential value of a network of "N" e-mail clients is greater than the potential value of a network of "N" fax machines as explained below. We can gain insight into the difference in value by comparing the key attributes of various information technologies, using the diagram portrayed in Figure A-2.

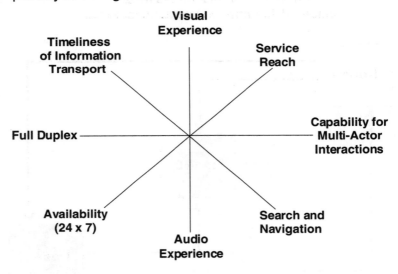

Figure A-2. Attributes of Information Technologies

As a point of departure, we can examine the key attributes of traditional mail, a very primitive "information technology," portrayed in Figure A-3. Mail can be sent and delivered to any address on the planet. In addition, large amounts of information, in customized format, can be sent by mail. Furthermore, we can observe that value to the "user" of mail service can be increased by decreasing the delivery time, as well as providing in-transit visibility (and return receipts).

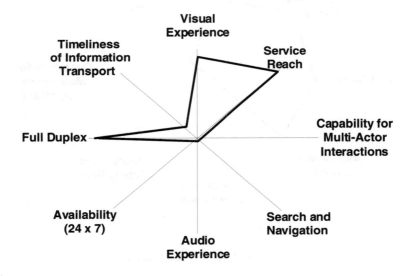

Figure A-3. Traditional Mail

Fax machines enable information "stored" in paper form to be digitized and transmitted in near-real time, resulting in drastically reduced delivery time compared to traditional mail, as shown in Figure A-4. However, faxes only can be sent to other fax machines, while traditional mail can be delivered to any "address" on the planet.

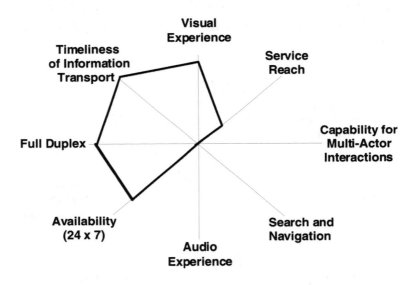

Figure A-4. Fax Machines

E-mail technology has some of same attributes as fax technology, as well as additional attributes. With e-mail, the potential exists for transmitting digital attachments, such as text files, graphic files, and audio files, as shown in Figure A-5. E-mail also allows messages to be stored electronically and easily referenced.

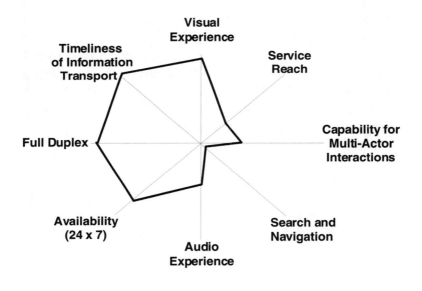

Figure A-5. E-Mail

However, in examining attributes associated with Web technologies, we can observe that this information technology enables fundamentally new types of information interactions, as portrayed in Figure A-6. Perhaps the most significant attribute is search and navigation. This attribute enables users to search for potential sources of information (via key word searches), and then navigate information sources once they are found. The capability for multi-actor interactions refers to the capability to enable multi-actor interactions, such as chat rooms, virtual white boards, and "on-line auctions" (e.g., eBay). *The capabilities enabled by the Web represent an order of magnitude increase in the ability of humans to operate in the information domain.*

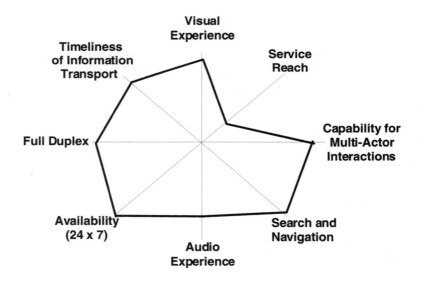

Figure A-6. World Wide Web

Clearly, the potential value of Web-enabled networked entities is greater than an equivalently sized network in which entities can interact via e-mail or fax. As was pointed out previously however, the value to the end user is a function of a user-value function, and a network-enabled, value-creation logic. Consequently, understanding the role that information interactions play in creating value (value-creation logic) is key to understanding the implications of Metcalfe's Law.

Now, given the complexity of the Internet and the potential for a large number of network-enabled, value-creation logics to be available to users, it becomes increasingly clear that it is virtually impossible to compute the "value" of a network to all end users or potential users. *However, it is possible for a single user, with a well-defined value metric, to estimate the potential value of the network to them as an individual user. Furthermore, it is also possible for the developers of Internet sites to identify the principle components of value for which customers may have a preference.*

Clearly, the process of computing value is complex. A useful approach is to recognize that attributes provide a basis for value, and that user preference, or utility, can be approximated as a weighing of attributes.

For example, consider the network-enabled, value-creation logic associated with on-line retailing for an Internet company such as Amazon.com. There are multiple potential attributes to the on-line experience, which are highlighted in Figure A-7, compared to traditional approaches. Individual customers will decide to participate in an on-line transaction to the extent that they place a "value" on these attributes. In some instances, individual attributes will be more or less important to the same customer.[8]

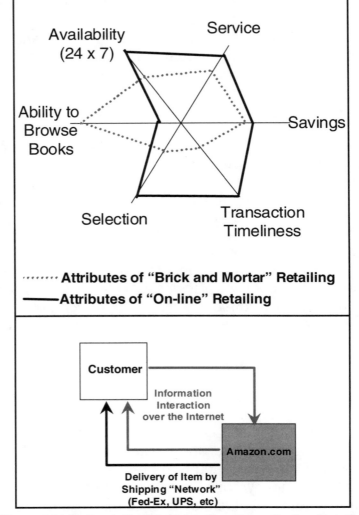

Figure A-7. Network-Centric Value Creation—On-line Retailing

---

[8] Leslie Walker, "Looking Beyond Books: Amazon's Bezos Sees Personalization as Key to Cyber-Stores' Future," *The Washington Post* (November 8, 1998, Section H: Business), 1, 14.

Similar trends hold with on-line stock trading, whose attributes are highlighted in Figure A-8. Now, as with on-line retailing, the value that an individual user will place on these attributes is a personal preference.

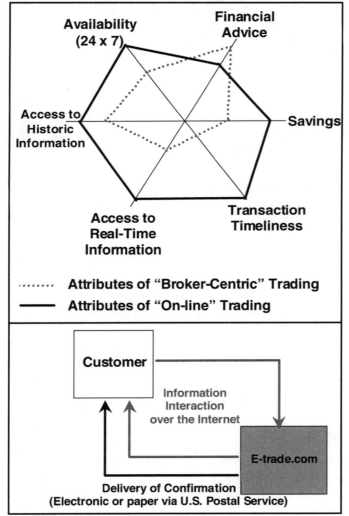

Figure A-8. Network-Centric Value Creation—On-line Trading

The key point here is to recognize that quantifying the value of a "network" requires both a value-creation logic and user-defined value preferences (value function). Consequently, in the domain of warfare, one should expect that similar logic would apply. Any measure of network-enabled combat power needs to have these two components: a value-creation logic and user-defined value preferences (value function).

The following examples of network-enabled (network-centric), value-creation logic in military operations provide insight into the sources of combat power associated with network-centric operations.

1) The networking of entities (sensors, deciders, actors) enables shared battlespace awareness. This shared awareness represents an improved position in the information domain.

2) High performance networking of sensors creates an improved position in the information domain by enabling sensor tasking and fusion, which decreases uncertainty associated with object state estimates: position, velocity, object identification (e.g., friendly, hostile).

3) Actors make decisions and "act" based on the content, quality, and timeliness of information in the information domain.

4) A position in the information domain is translated to combat power (measurable value) in the battlespace by actors and

decision makers. (Similar to the Internet, decisions made by actors are the source of value.)

5) Networking entities enables decision makers and actors to interact in new ways; in effect, to create new modes of operation. Self-synchronization is an example of a new, network-enabled mode of operation, or network-centric operation.

6) In addition, the networking of entities enables functions to be relocated, or reallocated, across the warfighting force.

In summary, the following can be said with respect to Metcalfe's Law:

To first order, it describes the potential number of information interactions that are enabled by a network of "N" nodes.

To second order, it provides insight into the fact that the "value" of a network to the users of the network is primarily a function of the interaction between:

1) content, quality, and timeliness of information interactions enabled by the network;
2) network-enabled, value-creation logic; and
3) user-value functions.

List of Acronyms

AEGIS – Advanced Electronic Guided Interceptor System

AFMSS – Air Force Mission Support System

AFSPACECOM – Air Force Space Command

ALERT – Attack and Launch Early Reporting to Theater

ATM – Asynchronous Transfer Mode

AWACS – Airborne Warning and Control System

AWE – Advanced Warfighting Experiment

BDA – Battlespace Damage Assessment

CCRP – C4ISR Cooperative Research Program

CD – Compact Disk

CEC – Cooperative Engagement Capability

CEP – Cooperative Engagement Processor

ConOps – Concept of Operations

COP – Common Operational Picture

DDS – Data Distribution System

DMG – Deutsche Morgan Grenfell, Inc.

DoD – Department of Defense

DOM – Doctrine, Organization, Materiel (ACOM's characterization)

DOTML-P – Doctrine, Organization, Training, Materiel, Leadership, and Personnel

dRAM – Dynamic Random Access Memory

DSP – Defense Support Program

EA – Evolutionary Acquisition

EFX – Expeditionary Force Experiment

ELINT – Electronic Intelligence

FAC – Forward Air Controller

FBE – Fleet Battle Experiment

GPS – Global Positioning System

GTN – Global Transportation Network

HARM – High-Speed Anti-Radiation Missile

HEAT – Headquarters Effectiveness Assessment Tool

IP – Internet Protocol

ISX – Information Superiority Experiment

IT – Information Technology

JAOC – Joint Air Operations Center

JIVA – Joint Intelligence Virtual Architecture

JSEAD – Joint Suppression of Enemy Air Defenses

JSTARS – Joint Surveillance Target Attack Radar System

JV2010 – Joint Vision 2010

LAMPS – Light Airborne Multi-Purpose System

MCP – Mission Capability Package

NCW – Network Centric Warfare

NGO – Non-Government Organization

NIPRNET – Sensitive but Unclassified Internet Protocol Router Network

OODA – Observation, Orientation, Decision, Action

OOTW – Operations Other Than War

PBX – Private Branch Exchange

OSD – Office of the Secretary of Defense

PCMR – Probability of Correct Message Receipt

PDA – Personal Digital Assistant

PVO – Private Voluntary Organization

SAM – Surface-to-Air Missile

SBIRS – Space-Based Infra Red System

SEAD – Suppression of Enemy Air Defenses

SIGINT – Signals Intelligence

SIPRNET – Secret Internet Protocol Router Network

SOF – Special Operations Forces

TCP/IP – Transmission Control Protocol/ Internet Protocol

UAV – Unmanned Aerial Vehicle

USJFCOM – United States Joint Forces Command

VTC – Video Teleconferencing

WMD – Weapons of Mass Destruction

Bibliography

AFCEA Study Team. *Evolutionary Acquisition Study.* Fairfax, VA: AFCEA, June 7, 1993.

Air Force Space Command/Space Warfare Center. *Information Briefing on Capabilities of Space Warfare Center/Shield Program.* Colorado Springs, CO, 1998.

Alberts, David S. *Command and Control in Peace Operations.* Washington, DC: National Defense University Press, 1995.

Alberts, David S. *Lessons Learned from ISX 1.1.* AIAA Joint Experiment Task Force Briefing, January 28, 1999.

Alberts, David S. *Operations Other Than War: The Technological Dimension.* Washington, DC: National Defense University Press, 1995.

Alberts, David S. *The Unintended Consequences of Information Age Technologies.* Washington, DC: National Defense University Press, 1996.

Alberts, David S., and Thomas J. Czerwinski. "Working Bibliography" in *Complexity, Global Politics, and National Security.* Washington, DC: National Defense University Press, 1997.

Alberts, David S., and Richard E. Hayes. *Command Arrangements for Peace Operations.* Washington, DC: National Defense University Press, 1995.

Allard, Kenneth. *Command, Control, and the Common Defense*, revised edition. Washington, DC: National Defense University Press, 1996.

Allard, Kenneth. *Somalia Operations: Lessons Learned.* Washington, DC: National Defense University Press, 1995.

Bond, BG William L., USA. *Army Digitization Overview.* Briefing to Dr. Jacques Gansler, USD (A&T). Pentagon, Arlington, VA, May 20, 1998.

Bond, BG William L., USA. *Military CIS '98.* Briefing to Dr. Jacques Gansler, USD (A&T). Pentagon, Arlington, VA, April 20, 1998.

Buchholz, LTG Douglas D., USA. Written testimony to hearing on defense transformation. Senate Armed Services Committee, subcommittee on airland forces, March 4, 1998.

Capitalizing on Innovation. Capital One's 1998 Debt Equity Conference, October 20, 1998.

Carroll, Christopher J., Managing Director, Head of Global Electronic Trading. Deutsche Morgan Grenfell, Inc., 1996-1997. Interviews.

Cebrowski, VAdm Arthur K., USN. "Network Centric Warfare: An Emerging Military Response to the Information Age." Presentation to the 1999 Command and Control Research and Technology Symposium, Naval War College, Newport, RI, June 29, 1999.

Cebrowski, VAdm Arthur K., USN. Written testimony to hearing on Defense Information Superiority and Information Assurance—Entering the 21st Century. House Armed Services Committee, subcommittee on military research and development and subcommittee on military procurement, February 23, 1999.

Cebrowski, VAdm Arthur K., USN, and John J. Garstka. "Network Centric Warfare: Its Origin and Future." *Proceedings of the Naval Institute* 124:1 (January 1998): 28–35.

CIO Imperative: Business Results Are the End— Information Sharing Is the Means. The Concours Group, 1997.

Clemins, Adm Archie R., USN. "Naval Simulation System (NSS): An Assessment of IT-21 Warfighting Value-Added." Briefing, January 5, 1999.

Cliffe, Sarah. "Knowledge Management: The Well-Connected Business." *Harvard Business Review* 76:4 (July-August 1998): 17–21.

Czerwinski, Tom. *Coping with the Bounds: Speculations on Nonlinearity in Military Affairs.* Washington, DC: National Defense University Press, 1998.

d'Estang, Valerie-Anne Giscard and Mark Young. *Inventions and Discoveries 1993.* New York: Facts on File, 1993.

Dockerty, John T. and A. E .R. Woodcock. *The Military Landscape: Mathematical Models of Combat.* Cambridge, UK: Woodhead, 1993.

Executive Summary of Global '98 Wargame. Report of wargame conducted at Naval War College, Newport, RI, July 13–31, 1998.

Foley, John. "Squeezing More Value from Data." *Information Week* (December 9, 1996): 44.

Frankel, Michael S., and Robert H. Gormley. "Achieving Information Dominance: The Integrated Information Infrastructure—A Vision for the 21st Century." *SRI International Study Report.* September 17, 1998.

Fulghum, David A. "Improved Air Defenses Prompt Pentagon Fears." *Aviation Week & Space Technology* 149:1 (July 6, 1998): 22–24.

Gell-Mann, Murray. *The Quark and the Jaguar.* New York: W.H. Freeman, 1994.

"George Gilder's Telecosm: Metcalfe's Law and Legacy." *Forbes ASAP* 152: Supplement (September 13, 1993): 158–166.

Goodden, R. Thomas, et al. *Education Technology in Support of Joint Professional Military Education in 2010: The EdTech Report.* Washington, DC: A Joint Staff Publication, October 1998.

Gore, John. *Chaos, Complexity, and the Military.* Washington, DC: National Defense University Press, 1996.

Hammes, T. X. "War Isn't a Rational Business." *Proceedings of the Naval Institute* 124:7 (July 1998): 22–35.

Hayes, Margaret Daly, and Gary F. Wheatley. *Interagency and Political-Military Dimensions of Peace Operations: Haiti—A Case Study.* Washington, DC: National Defense University Press, 1996.

Horner, Gen. Charles A., USAF (Ret.). "Comments on Expeditionary Force Experiment '98." *C2 Earlybird: Special Edition EFX 98 Lessons Learned.* 1: Special Ed. 1 (December 1998).

Hough, Richard, and Denis Richards. *The Battle of Britain: The Greatest Air Battle of World War II.* New York: W. W. Norton and Company, 1989.

James, Glenn E. *Chaos Theory: The Essentials for Military Applications.* Newport Paper 10. Newport, RI: Naval War College, 1996.

Johnson, Adm Jay L., USN. Address at the U.S. Naval Institute Annapolis Seminar and 123rd Annual Meeting, Annapolis, MD, April 23, 1997.

Johnson, Adm Jay L., USN. CNO Address at AFCEA West, San Diego, CA, January 21, 1998.

Knowledge and Speed: The Annual Report on the Army After Next Project to the Chief of Staff of the Army, July 1997.

Landa, Manuel de. *War in the Age of Intelligent Machines.* New York: Zone Books, 1991.

Libicki, Martin C. "DBK and Its Consequences." In *Dominant Battlespace Knowledge,* eds. Stuart E. Johnson and Martin C. Libicki, 23–49. Washington, DC: National Defense University Press, 1995.

Libicki, Martin C. *What Is Information Warfare?* Washington, DC: National Defense University Press, 1995.

Lorenz, Edward N. *The Essence of Chaos.* Seattle, WA: University of Washington Press, 1993.

Magretta, Joan. "The Power of Virtual Integration: An Interview with Dell Computer's Michael Dell." *Harvard Business Review* 76:2 (March–April 1998): 72–84.

Maurer, Martha. *Coalition Command and Control: Key Considerations.* Washington, DC: National Defense University Press, 1994.

McGrail, RAdm Charles R., USN (Ret.). Interviews, 1996–1998.

McNab, Andy. *Bravo Two Zero*. New York: Island Books, 1994.

Measuring the Effects of Network-Centric Warfare (Draft, Unpublished). Office of the Secretary of Defense (Net Assessment), Pentagon, Arlington, VA.

Mooney, Stephen C. *The Cyberstate*. Denver, CO: ACM, Inc., 1996.

Moore, James F. *The Death of Competition: Leadership and Strategy in the Age of Business Ecosystems*. New York: HarperBusiness, 1996.

Muller, David A., et al. "The electronic structure at the atomic scale of ultrathin gate oxides." *Nature*, Volume 399 (June 24, 1999): 758-761.

Murphy, Michael. *Every Investors Guide to High-Tech Stocks and Mutual Funds*. New York: Broadway Books, 1997.

"Naval Tactical C3 Architecture," 1985–1995. *Signal* 33:10 (August 1979): 71–72.

Newcomb, Peter. "The First Billion Takes a Lifetime...Except in the Internet Age." *Forbes* 163:8 (April 19, 1999): 246–247.

Nutwell, Robert M. "IT-21 Provides Big 'Reachbacks'." *Proceedings of the Naval Institute* 124:1 (January 1998): 36–38.

Palmeri, Christopher. "Believe in Yourself, Believe in the Merchandise." *Forbes* 160:5 (September 8, 1997): 118–124.

Phelan, Robert G., Jr., and Michael L. McGinnis. "Reengineering the United States Army's Tactical Command and Control Operational Architecture for Information Operations." *Proceedings of the 1996 Winter Simulation Conference*, 1996.

Porter, Michael E. *Competitive Advantage: Creating and Sustaining Superior Performance*. New York: Free Press, 1985.

Roca, Rich. "AT&T Bell Labs Presentation on Information Technology Trends to GovTechNet '99." Washington, DC, June 16, 1999.

Sabbagh, Karl. *Twenty-First Century Jet: The Making and Marketing of the Boeing 777*. New York: Scribner, 1996.

Schiesel, Seth. "Jumping Off the Bandwidth Wagon: Long Distance Carriers Regroup." *The New York Times* (July 3, 1999, Section 3: Money & Business): 1, 10, 11.

Schiesel, Seth. "The No. 1 Customer: Sorry It Isn't You." *The New York Times* (November 23, 1997, Section 3: Money & Business): 1, 10.

Schifrin, Matthew, and Erika Brown. "Merrill's Malaise." *Forbes* 163:7 (April 5, 1999): 108–114.

Sensor to Shooter III: Precision Engagement C4ISR Architecture Analysis, Final Report. Washington, DC: C4ISR Decision Support Center and Joint Chiefs of Staff Directorate for C4 Systems, June 15, 1997.

Sensor-to-Shooter C4 Battle Management, Final Report. Washington, DC: C4ISR Decision Support Center and Joint Chiefs of Staff Directorate for C4 Systems, April 1, 1999.

Siegel, Pascale Combelles. *Target Bosnia: Integrating Information Activities in Peace Operations.* Washington, DC: National Defense University Press, 1998.

Smart Card in Cobra Gold '98: Business Case Analysis—Final Report, Department of Defense Smart Card Technology Office, [http://www.dmdc.osd.mil/smartcard]. January 1999.

Sontag, Sherry, and Christopher Drew. *Blind Man's Bluff: The Untold Story of American Submarine Espionage.* Public Affairs™, 1998.

Stabel, Charles B., et al. "Configuring Value for Competitive Advantage: On Chains, Shops, and Networks." *Strategic Management Journal* 19 (1998): 413–437.

Stern, Carl W. "The Deconstruction of Value Chains." *Perspectives.* The Boston Consulting Group, September 1998.

Stevens, William K. "Naval Simulation System: Representation of Network Centric Warfare Concepts and Architectures." *Proceedings of the SMi Conference on Network Centric Warfare*, June 23-24, 1999, London.

Swoboda, Frank. "Talking Management with Chairman Welch." *The Washington Post* (March 23, 1997, Section H: Business): 1, 7.

Tactics, Techniques, and Procedures for the Common Operational Modeling, Planning, and Simulation Strategy (COMPASS), Version 1.1. JWID Joint Project Office, August 31, 1998.

Tapscott, Don. *The Digital Economy: Promise and Peril in the Age of Networked Intelligence.* New York: McGraw-Hill, 1996.

"The Cooperative Engagement Capability." *Johns Hopkins APL Technical Digest* 16:4 (1995): 377–396.

"The Leaders in 1997 Sales and Profits." *Business Week* 3567 (March 2, 1998): 110.

Tirpak, John A. "Deliberate Force." *Air Force.* 80:10 (October 1987).

Ullman, Harlan, James Wade, Jr., et al. *Shock and Awe: Achieving Rapid Dominance*. Washington, DC: National Defense University Press, 1996.

U.S. Air Force. *The Army Air Forces in World War II— Vol. I: Plans and Operations, January 1939–August 1942*. Chicago: University of Chicago Press, 1948.

U.S. Air Force. *The Army Air Forces in World War II— Vol. III: Argument to VE Day, January 1944–May 1945*. Office of Air Force History (1983 reprint): (Originally published University of Chicago Press, Chicago, 1948–1958).

U.S. Department of Commerce. "IT Industries—Of Growing Importance to the Economy and Jobs." Appendix 1 in *The Emerging Digital Economy*. Washington, DC: Government Printing Office.

U.S. Marine Corps. *Beyond C2: A Concept for Comprehensive Command and Coordination of the Marine Air-Ground Task Force*. Washington, DC: Headquarters, U.S. Marine Corps, June 2, 1998.

Waldrop, M. Mitchell. *Complexity: The Emerging Science at the Edge of Chaos*. New York: Simon and Schuster, 1992.

Walker, Leslie. "Looking Beyond Books: Amazon's Bezos Sees Personalization as Key to Cyber-Stores' Future." *The Washington Post* (November 8, 1998, Section H: Business): 1, 14.

Wallace, MG William S., USA, CG 4th ID, Fort Hood, TX. Interview, January 20, 1999.

Welch, Joseph A., Jr. "State of the Art of C2 Assessment." *Proceedings for Quantitative Assessment of the Utility of Command and Control System,* MTR 80W00025 (January 1980): 11.

Wentz, Larry. *Lessons from Bosnia: The IFOR Experience.* Washington, DC: National Defense University Press, 1998.

Willner, Alan E. "Mining the Optical Bandwidth for a Tera Bit Per Second." *IEEE Spectrum* (April 1997): 32-41.

Wurman, Richard Saul. *Information Anxiety.* New York: Bantam Books, 1990.

Woodward, Lt.Gen. John L., USAF. Written testimony to hearing on Defense Information Superiority and Information Assurance—Entering the 21st Century. House Armed Services Committee, subcommittee on military research and development and subcommittee on military procurement, February 23, 1999.

About the Authors

Dr. Alberts is currently the Director, Research OASD (C3I). He previously was the Director, Information Systems Engineering at the MITRE Corporation, a federally funded research and development center. Prior to this he was the Director, Advanced Concepts, Technologies, and Information Strategies (ACTIS), Deputy Director of the Institute for National Strategic Studies, and the executive agent for DoD's Command and Control Research Program. This included responsibility for the Center for Advanced Concepts and Technology (ACT) and the School of Information Warfare and Strategy (SIWS) at the National Defense University. He has more than 25 years of experience developing and introducing leading edge technology into private and public sector organizations. This extensive applied experience is augmented by a distinguished academic career in computer science and operations research, and Government service in senior policy and management positions.

John J. Garstka is currently the Scientific and Technical Advisor, Directorate for C4 Systems, Joint Chiefs of Staff (JCS/J6). In this capacity he is responsible for a broad range of issues associated with Information Superiority and Network Centric Warfare. In addition to co-authoring, with Vice Admiral Cebrowski, *Network Centric Warfare—Its Origin and Future* (Proceedings of the U.S. Naval Institute, January 1998), he has presented over 225 briefings on NCW to industry, DoD, and at international conferences. Prior to joining the JCS, Mr. Garstka led consulting assignments for Cambridge Research Associates and served as an Officer in the U.S. Air Force, with assignments at the Pentagon and U.S. Air Force Space Systems Division. He is a Distinguished Graduate of the U.S. Air Force Academy and studied as a Hertz Fellow at Stanford University, where he earned an M.S. in Engineering-Economic Systems. Mr. Garstka is also currently an officer in the U.S. Air Force Reserve.

COL (ret) Fred Stein served 27 years in the U.S. Army supporting tactical and operational level forces. He commanded the 7th Signal Brigade during *Operation Support Hope* and acted as the J6 in both Rwanda and Bosnia for joint and combined operations. During service with the J6 Joint Chiefs of Staff, he assisted in the development of the Joint Battle Center and the Decision Support Center. He was the J6 lead in the Communications Mission Analysis (CMA) presented to the Joint Requirements Oversight Committee (JROC) at the last Quadrennial Defense Review. Publications include papers on Bosnia Communications Support, Low Intensity Computation and Communications Support, and Network Centric Warfare. COL (ret) Stein worked for Evidence Based Research while working on this book, and is now located at FT Hood, Texas, serving as the senior MITRE representative to III Corps in support of the first digitized Division and Corps.

1994 - Present

Order Form

Title_____Name_____
Company_____
Address_____
City_____State____Zip_____Country_____

ALLOW 4 TO 6 WEEKS FOR DELIVERY

Quantity	CCRP Publication Series	CCRP Use Only
	Command, Control, and the Common Defense	D4699
	Command and Control in Peace Operations	D4990
	Command Arrangements for Peace Operations	95743
	Complexity, Global Politics, and National Security	D4946
	Coping with the Bounds	94115B
	Behind the Wizard's Curtain	95015
	Dominant Battlespace Knowledge	95743D
	Information Age Anthology Vol. I	93339
	Information Age Anthology Vol. II	FUTURE
	Information Warfare and International Law	94115A
	The Mesh and the Net	93339A
	Network Centric Warfare (1st)	D6033
	Network Centric Warfare (2nd)	722-916
	Standards: The Rough Road to the Common Byte	93339B
	The Unintended Consequences of Information Age Technologies	95743A
	Confrontation Analysis	723-125
	Doing Windows	D4698
	Humanitarian Assistance and Disaster Relief in the Next Century	D6192
	Information Campaigns for Peace Operations	FUTURE
	Interagency and Political-Military Dimensions of Peace Operations: Haiti	95743C
	Lessons from Bosnia	94115
	1998/4th Int'l CCRTS CD-ROM	CD98
	1999 CCRTS CD-ROM	CD99

Order # _____
CCRP Use Only

FAX COVER SHEET

CCRP publications are available at no cost through DoD. Complete the order form on the reverse side and fax the sheets or mail to c/o address below.

To:	Publications Coordinator
Fax:	(703) 821-7742
E-mail:	ccrp_pubs@ebrinc.com

From:
Telephone:
Fax:
E-mail:
Date:
Pages: 02

Additional Information: